REVOLUTION

Volume 7

CREATIVE REVOLUTION

CREATIVE REVOLUTION

A Study of Communist Ergatocracy

EDEN AND CEDER PAUL

LONDON AND NEW YORK

First published in 1920 by George Allen & Unwin Ltd.

This edition first published in 2022
by Routledge
4 Park Square, Milton Park, Abingdon, Oxon OX14 4RN

and by Routledge
605 Third Avenue, New York, NY 10158

Routledge is an imprint of the Taylor & Francis Group, an informa business

© 1920 Eden and Ceder Paul

All rights reserved. No part of this book may be reprinted or reproduced or utilised in any form or by any electronic, mechanical, or other means, now known or hereafter invented, including photocopying and recording, or in any information storage or retrieval system, without permission in writing from the publishers.

Trademark notice: Product or corporate names may be trademarks or registered trademarks, and are used only for identification and explanation without intent to infringe.

British Library Cataloguing in Publication Data
A catalogue record for this book is available from the British Library

ISBN: 978-1-032-12623-4 (Set)
ISBN: 978-1-003-26095-0 (Set) (ebk)
ISBN: 978-1-032-12747-7 (Volume 7) (hbk)
ISBN: 978-1-032-12749-1 (Volume 7) (pbk)
ISBN: 978-1-003-22606-2 (Volume 7) (ebk)

DOI: 10.4324/9781003226062

Publisher's Note
The publisher has gone to great lengths to ensure the quality of this reprint but points out that some imperfections in the original copies may be apparent.

Disclaimer
The publisher has made every effort to trace copyright holders and would welcome correspondence from those they have been unable to trace.

Creative Revolution

A Study of
Communist Ergatocracy

By

Eden & Cedar Paul

*Revolution is the highest form of creation,
the re-creation of the animate matter of
the social organism.*
              J. R. WHITE.

LONDON : GEORGE ALLEN & UNWIN LTD.
RUSKIN HOUSE, 40 MUSEUM STREET, W.C. 1

First published in 1920

(All rights reserved)

To

Vladimir Ilich Ulianov

commonly known as

Lenin

Chairman of the People's Commissaries

of the

Russian Socialist Federative Soviet Republic

TABLE OF CONTENTS

CHAPTER ONE

PAGE

COMMUNIST ERGATOCRACY. 11

CHAPTER TWO

SOCIALISM THROUGH SOCIAL SOLIDARITY . . . 27

CHAPTER THREE

SOCIALISM THROUGH THE CLASS STRUGGLE . . 45

CHAPTER FOUR

THE SHOP STEWARDS' MOVEMENT . . . 63

CHAPTER FIVE

HISTORICAL SIGNIFICANCE OF THE GREAT WAR . . 83

CHAPTER SIX

THE RUSSIAN REVOLUTION 97

CHAPTER SEVEN

THE THIRD INTERNATIONAL 111

8   CREATIVE REVOLUTION

CHAPTER EIGHT

PAGE

The Dictatorship of the Proletariat . . 129

CHAPTER NINE

The Iron Law of Oligarchy 147

CHAPTER TEN

Socialism through Parliament or Soviet? . . 165

CHAPTER ELEVEN

Creative Revolution 183

CHAPTER TWELVE

Freedom 203

Bibliography 219

CHAPTER ONE

COMMUNIST ERGATOCRACY

The political and social aim of democracy is to abolish a relationship of subjection and rule. The derivative meaning of the term democracy is " people's rule." Modern democracy does not aim at *rule* at all, but at *administration* ; at the administration of the people, by the people, for the people. How this new conception, this new estimate, of state organisation can be carried out in practice is no mere question of power ; it is a difficult problem of *administrative technique.*

T. G. MASARYK.

CHAPTER ONE

COMMUNIST ERGATOCRACY

THIS little volume has a twofold aim, theoretical and practical. In the theoretical field, we wish to effect an analysis of socialist trends and to attempt a synthesis of contemporary proletarian aims. In the sphere of practice, we hope to intensify and to liberate the impulse towards a fresh creative effort. The philosophy we expound is the philosophy of ergatocracy, a new term of which no succinct definition can be given on the first page. The need for definition, and the impossibility of defining ergatocracy in a pithy phrase, has impelled the production of a booklet; and nothing but the urgency of the hour, coupled perhaps with our temperamental disinclination for Teutonic thoroughness, has prevented the booklet from attaining the proportions and ponderosity of a treatise, documented, as the French say, with innumerable citations, and bristling with footnotes. Yet in the case of so new a word—it is little more than a year since it was launched upon a reluctant world, and it does not yet enjoy the hospitality of any dictionary —some attempt at definition is needed at the very outset. The lack of a new name to denote

12 CREATIVE REVOLUTION

the new political philosophy of left-wing socialists has been manifest for some years. We have been moving away from the old conceptions of democracy. Syndicalism, which, as a counter-blast to statism and parliamentary labourism, flourished in the years immediately preceding the war, was one of several attempts to restate socialist criticism, socialist aims, and the methods of socialist reconstruction. Statism, syndicalism, guild socialism, and various other competing "isms," will receive due attention in the sequel. For the moment it will suffice to justify the coining of the term "ergatocracy," and to give a brief indication of its significance.

Until quite recently, all forward spirits have imagined themselves to be moving "Towards Democracy." Now democracy (like ergatocracy) is a temperament, a habit of mind, an outlook on life, quite as much as an abstract political philosophy; it is no mere product of the pure understanding, but is deeply tinged with feeling, impulse, and desire; consequently, we are unjust to the concept "democracy" if we attempt to confine its soaring pinions within the cage of a narrow intellectualist formula. The poetically minded democrat wishes to fly sunward, to pulse athwart the empyrean with Shelley and with Whitman. But when we come to *reason* about our conceptions, we must fold our wings and take our stand on the solid earth; the intelligence must operate with the sober methods of comparatively unmetaphorical prose. The democrat must content himself with some such

COMMUNIST ERGATOCRACY 13

formula as " Democracy is the government of the people, for the people, by the people." Mallock, a shrewd critic, in the opening chapter of *The Limits of Pure Democracy*, has little difficulty in exposing the hollowness of this famous phrase. But it conveniently expresses what most people mean, or think they mean, by democracy ; and at this stage of our argument it will be useful to employ a similar phrase in preliminary explanation of the term ergatocracy. As usual in modern English, the coiner of a neologism must have recourse to the rich and expressive language of the Greeks. " Democracy " was once a new word, and probably aroused the hostility of misoneists among the contemporaries of Pericles when, using the word-building resources of their own tongue, certain Greeks who felt the need of a new name for a new idea, linked together the words *demos*, people, and *kratia*, rule or government, to make *demokratia*, democracy, people's rule, or popular government. " Ergatocracy " is formed on precisely similar lines. *Ergates* is the Greek word for " worker." The second component of the new term, " cracy," is unchanged in form, but is destined, we conceive, to undergo a gradual change in meaning. During the phase of revolutionary transition, as will be made clear in the chapter on " The Dictatorship of the Proletariat," ergatocracy will unquestionably signify " workers' rule " ; there will have to be a highly centralised governmental authority, exercising *rule* in the strictest sense. The expropriators

14   CREATIVE REVOLUTION

will not submit tamely when the screw-press of expropriation is applied to them in their turn. Despite the diffusion of a revolutionary mass - psychology, which alone (such is our belief) will render the change to socialism possible, large sections of the lower middle class will stubbornly cling to the wreckage of the old order. Undoubtedly, too, large sections even of the urban proletariat and perhaps a majority of the rural proletariat will waver in loyalty to the new system, above all in such a country as Britain, more dependent than any other on foreign lands for the necessaries of life, and one therefore in which the transition will perhaps be marked by a period of exceptional hardship. All these recalcitrant elements may have to be " governed " somewhat strenuously by the dominant class-conscious proletariat. But the aim of socialism is to abolish the relationship of subjection and rule. As communist ergatocracy realises itself in practice ; as the socialist mentality becomes generalised under socialist institutions ; when the ownership rule which is the essential characteristic of bourgeois " democracy " has been destroyed beyond all possibility of revival ; when the government of men has been replaced by the administration of things— then, with the passing of the phase of the dictatorship of the proletariat, the connotation of the " cracy " element in the term ergatocracy, will suffer a sea-change. Thus, whereas the dictatorship of the proletariat involves the substitution of the power of one class for the power

COMMUNIST ERGATOCRACY 15

of another, the replacement of bourgeois oligarchy by working-class rule—when class shall have been abolished once for all, we shall have attained our more immediate goal, we shall have passed through dictatorship to ergatocracy. And ergatocracy, to paraphrase the formula previously quoted, will signify the administration of the workers, for the workers, by the workers. Since all, except the immature, the retired, and the incapacitated, will then be active workers, there will be no class rule. Ergatocracy has many additional implications. Each chapter will be a fresh attempt to unfold and to elucidate one or more of these. But as a preliminary definition, the brief formula must suffice.

Before passing to other definitions that seem expedient at this stage, a word must be said in further justification of the neologism. A much fuller justification will become apparent in the course of our criticism of democracy. At the moment we may content ourselves with pointing to the confusionism that results from the way in which those who are really ergatocrats, those who frankly repudiate the democracy of Lloyd George and Woodrow Wilson, continue to label themselves democrats while endeavouring to distinguish their position by prefixing some qualifying adjective. Augustin Hamon coined one of the best of these hybrids when he wrote to us the other day that in a work he was planning he hoped to show that what we call ergatocracy is really a "sublimated

16 CREATIVE REVOLUTION

democracy." Some talk of "true democracy";
and others of "genuine" or "veritable democracy," which, as by a conjuring trick, is to be
substituted for the various counterfeits for which
the world has been made safe by five years of
war. This time there is to be no deception!
Lenin, in his speech on the Third International
delivered in Moscow on April 15, 1919, endeavoured to draw a distinction between "proletarian democracy" and "bourgeois democracy."
Again and again, in *The State and Revolution*
and other writings, he sings the praises of
"proletarian democracy." To all these good
comrades we would say, after the steam-roller
manner of Bohun in *You Never Can Tell*:
"Stop talking about democracy. You think
you are democrats, but you are not. You think
you want democracy, but you don't. You are
ergatocrats and you want ergatocracy. Democracy is the method of the outworn era of
capitalism, and 'democracy' is a term that
has been soiled by all ignoble use. Leave democracy to the liberal bourgeoisie and to the
Laodiceans among the socialists. Your objective
is ergatocracy."

This volume is a study of communist ergatocracy. Is a distinction then to be drawn between
"socialism" and "communism"? To a certain
extent, yes, as will be shown by-and-by. But
the distinction is rather one of atmosphere and
method than of doctrinal content. Strangely
apposite to-day are the words which Engels
used in the preface to the 1888 English edition

COMMUNIST ERGATOCRACY 17

of the *Manifesto of the Communist Party*. The manifesto is, he declares, a *communist* manifesto. " We could not have called it a socialist manifesto. By ' socialists,' in 1847, were understood . . . men outside the working-class movement, and looking rather to the ' educated ' classes for support. Whatever portion of the working class had become convinced of the insufficiency of a mere political revolution, and had proclaimed the necessity of a total social change, that portion, then, called itself ' communist.' . . . Socialism was, in 1847, a middle-class movement ; communism a working-class movement. Socialism was, on the continent at least, ' respectable ' ; communism was the very opposite. And as our notion, from the beginning, was that ' the emancipation of the working class must be the act of the working class itself,' there could be no doubt as to which of the two names we must take. Moreover, we have, ever since, been far from repudiating it."

During the forty years that had elapsed between the issue of the *Communist Manifesto* and the writing of the above-quoted preface, the distinction between socialism and communism had become blurred. Thirty years more were to intervene before, with the occurrence of a working-class economic revolution in Russia (November, 1917) calling itself " communist," followed a year later (November, 1918) by a largely middle-class political revolution in Germany calling itself " socialist," the distinction between socialism and communism was once

18 CREATIVE REVOLUTION

again to become conspicuous. The difference was underlined in March, 1919, when the Third International was founded at Moscow. Since then, the communist left wing has throughout the world been marked off more and more sharply from the socialist centre and right wing. " Socialism " to-day is pink, semi-bourgeois, and respectable ; " communism " is red, proletarian, disreputable, and bolshevist. But throughout the intervening years, for nearly three-quarters of a century, the terms socialist and communist have been almost interchangeable ; while the use of the expressions " socialism " and " socialist " has predominated. In discussing the general philosophy of the movement during these years, we should darken counsel were we to import into the argument a contrast which had for the time passed into abeyance. Further, at the hour when we write, the divergence between the two wings of the movement depends quite as much upon sources of inspiration, class asso- ciations, and the characteristics of class aims, as upon doctrinal differences. The philosophy and the trend of right-wing socialism are sub- stantially middle class. Left-wing socialism, on the other hand, is fundamentally proletarian. Enough ! The definition requisite at this point is the definition of " socialism."

Socialism is far from easy to define. Socialism, though it is a thing or rather an abstraction, we have been talking about for a century, though it is something to which myriads have devoted the best energies of the best years of

COMMUNIST ERGATOCRACY 19

their lives, is still in the making, and still in the earliest stages of that making. Creative evolution, as the right wing thinks, and creative revolution, as the left wing thinks, has still to work upon the developing plasma, has still to fashion the splendid limbs of the growing organism. It lies still shrouded within the womb of time ; we cannot drag it forth prematurely, examine all its characteristics, determine its limits with precision. It exists only in the realm of mind—or at least, prior to November, 1917, it existed only in the realm of mind. And as a mental entity, it exists quite as much in the realm of art and feeling, in the realm of impulse and desire, as in the realm of reason or intellect. When we have created socialism, we shall know better what socialism is, than we can possibly know to-day. Socialism is still in the world of the unborn, the world of human conation, the world (as a Freudian might say) of the *libido*. To define socialism seems, at times, wellnigh as difficult as to realise socialism in practice. Yet a definition must be attempted.

Socialism, as we cannot fail to perceive when we study the history of the socialist movement, and when we analyse the idea as it exists within our own minds, has threefold roots in the three spheres into which, for convenience, the unity of the human psyche has been artifically divided. Intellectually, socialism is a criticism of the existing order ; emotionally and in the realm of art it is the feeling that we can replace that order by a better, by an order that shapes

20   CREATIVE REVOLUTION

itself in the imagination as the result of our intellectual criticism of capitalism ; volitionally, or in the realm of will, it is an endeavour to create in the world of objective fact what we have already conceived in the intellectual and artistic imagination. It is an endeavour to overthrow the capitalist order, that latest and most finished form of ownership rule, and to replace it by the rule, or better by the administration, of the workers. It is an attempt to put an end to exploitation, to the use of man or woman as a mere means to another's ends. It is a realisation, as far as the left wing of anarchising socialists is concerned, that the driving force in the revolution must in large measure be a refusal on the individual's part to allow himself to be exploited, to allow others to treat him as means and not as end. " Do not unto others what you would not they should do unto you," is an excellent, a golden maxim ; but no less excellent, no less golden, is its counterpart, " Resist the exploiter ! " Hence left-wing socialism has an anarchist subflavour. " Resist the exploiter, and he will flee from you ! "

Exploitation is the arch-enemy of mankind : the exploitation of the young by the old, and of the old by the young ; of men by women, and of women by men ; of the weak by the strong, and of the strong by the weak ; of the poor by the rich, and of the rich by the poor. Hostility to all these forms of exploitation is of the essence of socialism ; but for the nonce we have to concentrate upon economic exploita-

COMMUNIST ERGATOCRACY 21

tion, upon the exploitation of the dispossessed by the owners. Throughout history, from the days of primitive communism onwards, human society has been rooted in ownership rule. The change from chattel slavery to feudalism, the change from feudalism to capitalism, these were but partial revolutions, these were but substitutions of one form of ownership rule for another. The revolution known as socialist will be a complete revolution, which will once for all expel ownership rule from the world of human life. Chattel slavery, feudalism, the guild patriciates of the medieval city-states, and, last of all, capitalism, were based upon distinct methods of production ; and in each of them the means of production were owned by a different type of ruling class. Socialism will be based upon yet another method of production, will be based upon self-government in industry ; this will involve the final disappearance of ownership rule, and therewith the final disappearance of class.

No more need be said, at this stage, concerning the meaning we attach to the word socialism. But its definition has necessitated the introduction of another debatable term, "revolution." The word has wide connotations, and in large part our booklet will be a discussion of those connotations, no less than of the connotations of " socialism," " communism," and " ergatocracy." But misconception may be obviated by a preliminary explanation. Engels uses the term as it is generally used by thoughtful revo-

CREATIVE REVOLUTION

lutionary socialists when he writes that "the working class had become convinced of the inefficiency of mere political revolution, and had proclaimed the necessity of a total social change." By revolution we mean an ostensibly rapid and very thorough change. Let us take a concrete example. The glacier flows slowly seaward and out into the sea. As it pushes onwards, tensions accumulate, for the downward trend of the glacier bed thrusts the ice beneath the water, and ice is lighter than water. Of a sudden, when the increasing stresses overcome the tenacity of the ice, a revolution occurs. To use the arctic sailors' metaphor, the glacier "calves." A huge block at the seaward end snaps off, and sails away as an iceberg. After a while, the iceberg drifts into a warm current, and slowly, very slowly, part of the great mass beneath the waves melts away ; the centre of gravity is gradually shifted ; at length, without warning, the iceberg turns topsy-turvy. Another revolutionary change ! Anyone who gets in the way of the calving glacier or the summersaulting iceberg is likely to be hurt ; the glacier does not *want*, the iceberg does not *want* a bloody revolution. Human beings are warmer than glaciers, warmer than icebergs ; and, in human society, revolutions are, to a preponderant extent at least, the outcome of the human will. Anyone who endeavours to resist the revolutionary will, may suffer for it. Yet no more than glacier or iceberg, do revolutionary socialists *desire* a bloody revolution. We should greatly prefer

COMMUNIST ERGATOCRACY 23

to effect our sudden, our revolutionary change by peaceful means. If there be bloodshed it will be because the reactionaries, the adherents of the old regime, the beneficiaries of the capitalist state, will employ all the forces of that state on behalf of what they term law and order. But cannot socialists peacefully gain control of the forces of law and order? Cannot they capture parliament by the use of the democratic suffrage, and then, having quietly voted the capitalists out of power, proceed, undisturbed by the turmoil of revolution, to establish the socialist commonwealth by legislative enactment at Westminster? Revolutionists though they termed themselves, such was for long periods and in one of their alternative moods, the belief of Marx and Engels. As from the gospels, so from Marx and Engels, the adherents of conflicting schools can readily select isolated passages which seem to justify their respective views by the *ipse dixit* of a master. "But they did not know everything down in Judee," and each generation must make its own contribution to the fires of human progress. The parliamentary method will be discussed from many points of view in later chapters. At the start we have to secure a general outlook upon the two main conflicting trends in the evolution of the socialist idea.

CHAPTER TWO

**SOCIALISM
THROUGH
SOCIAL
SOLIDARITY**

The Fabians . . . threw over the advocacy of revolution, the Marxian doctrine of value, and the class war. What remained was state socialism and a doctrine of " permeation."

BERTRAND RUSSELL.

The social organisation, like the body, is in a constant state of change and readaptation, responsive to every movement of the human intelligence, sensitive to every change in the mass will. . . . The Independent Labour Party . . . believes in the class conflict as a descriptive fact, but . . . does not regard it as supplying a political method. It strives to transform through education, through raising the standards of mental and moral qualities, through the acceptance of programmes by reason of their justice, rationality, and wisdom.

J. RAMSAY MACDONALD.

CHAPTER TWO

SOCIALISM THROUGH SOCIAL SOLIDARITY

ATTEMPTS have repeatedly been made to contrast two broadly divergent schools of socialist thought by the use of sharply adversative phrases. Long ago, Engels wrote of *The Development of Socialism from Utopia to Science*; whilst within the last few months, and perhaps with fuller justification, Radek has published a pamphlet entitled *The Development of Socialism from Science to Action*. Evolutionary and revolutionary socialism are frequently contrasted, and so are centralist or statist and decentralist or anarchising socialism. The "social democracy " of the Germans was, in part at least, a counterblast to the " aristocratic " state socialism of the Bismarckian era. To-day we have the nationalist socialism of the Hyndmans and the Hervés, the Blatchfords and the Scheidemanns, in sharp conflict with the internationalist socialism of the adherents of the Third International. " Direct action " versus " political action " is a familiar battle-cry. To-day the most notable line of cleavage, at any rate as far as tactics are concerned, would seem to be between the sovietists and the parliamentarians.

28 CREATIVE REVOLUTION

But just as in Great Britain we have a body like the Independent Labour Party combining a parliamentarian tactic leading in the direction of state socialism with a strongly anarchist or libertarian trend, and occupying a vague intermediate position between the Fabians and the left wing, so in France do we find the Socialist Party uttering the phraseology of revolutionary Marxism and the class struggle while it devotes its main energies to the capture of political power through parliament. Similar perplexities confront us everywhere, outside Russia, when we try to analyse contemporary socialist trends. Is it possible to throw any clear light upon all this confusion ? We believe it to be possible, and we hold that the issues have been marvellously clarified during the two years that have elapsed since the bolshevik revolution. In this and in the following chapter an attempt will be made to define the respective right-wing and left-wing characteristics, with especial reference to the British socialist movement, but gaining fresh illumination, as occasion serves, from foreign parallels.

The main line of distinction is suggested in the titles of this and the ensuing chapter : Socialism through Social Solidarity, and Socialism through the Class Struggle. For the purposes of this classification it is necessary to ignore the " centre." Those who are convinced that we are now in a revolutionary phase of social development, those who feel that the present is one of those supreme hours when

SOCIAL SOLIDARITY 29

it is essential to choose a side, are certainly entitled to contend that in the socialist movement to-day there is no place for a centre party. Since November, 1917, the left wing has had no use for anyone who wants to keep a foot in both camps, for anyone who wants to make the best of both worlds. *Creative Revolution* is an endeavour to clear much prevalent confusionism away from the path of socialist theory ; but it is likewise a call to arms, and is an expression of the belief that in the approaching struggle the " moderates " who pride themselves upon maintaining an impossibly " judicial " frame of mind will be nothing but an infernal nuisance to both parties—and will probably succumb to a cross fire. But substantially those who conceive themselves to belong to the centre are, spiritually and materially, children of the right wing.

The right wing believes that there exists to-day, in capitalist society, a working social solidarity. In conjunction with the Independent Labour Party (as its outlook and its aims are voiced by MacDonald), many adherents of the right wing may " believe in the class conflict as a descriptive fact," but they do not " believe in the class conflict as supplying a political method." Many again, like the Fabians, " throw over the advocacy of revolution, the Marxian doctrine of value, and the class war." A number of the shining lights of the parliamentary Labour Party explicitly repudiate the class conflict even as a descriptive fact.

80 CREATIVE REVOLUTION

They regard the doctrine as abominable, and are as outspoken champions of social solidarity as any Cobdenite liberal or true-blue tory among their habitual associates at Westminster. Pass by these extremists, "extremists" in the reactionary sense, and consider the typical exponents of the mentality of the right wing. Fabianism has lost the impetus, the fire, of its youthful days. There has not, as far as we are aware, been any recent pronouncement officially emanating from Fabian circles, any attempt to restate the Fabian policy in accordance with contemporary needs as modified by the war and the Russian revolution. Bernard Shaw's brilliancy as playwright and humorist is undimmed, but as sociologist he seems out of touch with the modern working-class movement, and in any case he has deliberately withdrawn from active participation in the counsels of the Fabian Society. Sidney Webb, however, remains on the executive of the Labour Party, and it is an open secret that the spirit of the Webbs, the finished expression of Fabianism, is the moving spirit of Labour Party policy. Bertrand Russell's description of Fabianism is penned by a critic of that school, but its accuracy will hardly be challenged. " In England," he wrote in 1916, " socialism has been inspired in the main by Fabianism." When, being far more thorough than the German revisionists, they had jettisoned every bale of the socialist cargo that was stamped with the Marxist stencil, there was nothing left that class-war socialists

SOCIAL SOLIDARITY 81

could easily recognise as socialism to-day. " What remained was state socialism and a doctrine of ' permeation.' Civil servants were to be permeated into the realisation that state socialism would enormously increase their power. Trade unions were to be permeated into the belief that the day for purely individual action was passed, and that they must look to government (inspired secretly by sympathetic civil servants) to bring about, bit by bit, such parts of the socialist programme as were not likely to arouse much hostility in the rich."

The Fabians, however, have invariably been socialist tacticians rather than socialist philosophers. The idea of permeation, which will ever remain associated with their name, was pre-eminently a tactical and not a philosophical conception. In so far as they had a philosophy at all it was the philosophy of Fabius Cunctator (the delayer), the philosophy of *festina lente* (more haste, less speed), the philosophy of " Bring socialism ; but not in our time O Lord ! " Obvious as it is that Fabian tactics, repudiating the class struggle, are based upon the belief that there is a real social solidarity to-day, upon the belief that the political institutions of bourgeoisdom are, or can be made, an effective expression of the needs of all classes conceived as forming part of an integral society, it is not to the Fabian tracts that the student turns for any coherent statement of such a philosophy. The conception of social solidarity as a basis of socialist progress finds its supreme expression in

32　CREATIVE REVOLUTION

Britain in the publications of the Independent Labour Party. At street corners, the working-class propagandists of that party often expound a colourable imitation of Marxist socialism ; but the official exponents of I.L.P. policy, and the official disseminators of I.L.P. philosophy, sing another tune. For a clear exposition of the social solidarity outlook, let us turn to the latest manifesto by one of the ablest and most courageous champions of that philosophy, let us turn to *Parliament and Revolution*. It speaks with no uncertain voice. " Parliament," writes Ramsay MacDonald, " being the will of the people embodied in an institution, socialists must work to get the right will and an intelligent will, and to provide the most intimate touch between the two. . . . Instead of harbouring designs to destroy representative government or to construct it on some basis other than democratic, socialists should consider how to perfect the system. . . . The social organisation, like the body, is in a constant state of change and of readaptation, responsive to every movement of the human intelligence, sensitive to every change in the mass will." And at the close of the work comes the passage already quoted at the head of this chapter. The mission of the I.L.P., says MacDonald, is " to transform through education, through raising the standards of mental and moral qualities, through the acceptance of programmes by reason of their justice, rationality, and wisdom."

These words give forceful expression to a view

SOCIAL SOLIDARITY 33

which conflicts radically with that of those who consider the Marxist criticism of capitalist society to be sound ; the view of those who believe that, under capitalism, social solidarity is a chimera, and that social solidarity cannot possibly be realised until we have passed through proletarian dictatorship to ergatocracy. The present writers are not fanatical devotees of " the gospel according to Karl Marx," and they think that along certain lines (where the interests of the ruling class are substantially unaffected, and in rare cases when the interests of all classes are genuinely identical) a considerable measure of social solidarity has at times been attained. But for the most part such achievements of social solidarity belonged to an earlier phase in the development of capitalist institutions. As capitalism draws nearer the nemesis that awaits it, the class struggle becomes accentuated, and rulers and ruled alike grow increasingly class conscious. Concomitantly with these changes, the state, parliament, the press, the system of " national " education, and all the diffused machinery for the manufacture of what is quaintly termed " public opinion," are devoted more and more deliberately to the service of reaction. This is called the maintenance of law and order, and the apostles of law and order are actuated by the most virtuous intentions in the world. The system by which they profit seems to them—we speak of typical members of the class, and ignore exceptions—if not the best of all conceivable systems, at least the

8

84 CREATIVE REVOLUTION

best system which poor human nature can work out. To revolutionaries, on the other hand, " law and order " tend increasingly, as the revolutionary phase grows more acute, to become synonymous with " reaction." Lester F. Ward, the American sociologist, drew attention to this remarkable antithesis many years ago in his *Dynamic Sociology*. " The party of order, in their love of order, come to hate progress, and regard it as the enemy of order. The party of progress, in their zeal for progress, come to detest order, and to regard it as the great enemy of progress." To-day the battle is once more joined between " order " and " progress " ; and to-day more than ever is the struggle, both ideological and material, one between rival classes.

The essence of the Marxist outlook is that the class struggle is the warp and woof of a society based on ownership rule, whether those who make up " society " are themselves aware of the fact or not. And the essence of the Marxist theory of reconstruction is that the nature of capitalist development leads to an increasing awareness of the class conflict, to an intensification of class-consciousness on both sides, culminating in a revolutionary explosion. To talk, under such conditions, of the " social organisation " being " responsive to every movement of the human intelligence " ; to assert that it is " sensitive to every change in the mass will " ; nay more, to talk, under such conditions, of " social organisation " and " mass

SOCIAL SOLIDARITY 85

will " at all, if the terms be conceived as applying to a hypothetical community-at-large unaffected by the volcanic dissensions of the class war—what is this but to play with words, to translate us into the fabled region of the absolute, where all contradictions are reconciled, where A and not-A are identical, where reasoners cease from troubling and logicians are at rest ? Assuredly MacDonald's own pacifist comrades in the I.L.P. would look askance at him were he to maintain that the " mass will " of war-making England during the period from August, 1914, down to the end of 1918, the mass will which returned the coalition government to power at the last general election, the mass will which insisted on the dismissal of Admiral Bacon because, in his public announcement concerning the destroyer action of April 20, 1917, he recorded that " fortunately " the force under his command had been able to save the lives of many Germans—were he to maintain that this mass will to which the social organisation responded with such admirable sensitiveness represented anything more subtle than the imagined interests of a group of capitalist imperialists and the herd-instincts of a war-maddened mob. MacDonald will retort, " I believe in the class conflict as a descriptive fact, though I do not regard it as supplying a political method. I admit that the war was, in part, a manifestation of the class conflict. But with regard to the evils to which you refer, I have explained, and you have quoted my

36   CREATIVE REVOLUTION

explanation, that the party to which I belong has a remedy for them all. It strives to transform through education, through raising the standards of mental and moral qualities, through the acceptance of programmes by reason of their rationality, justice, and wisdom." This introduces us to another profound difference between the socialist right and the socialist left.

The socialist right, the socialist champions of parliamentary institutions, and, above all, the members of the I.L.P. and those who hold similar conceptions of the dynamic of social reconstruction, are committed to an obsolete psychology, the characteristic psychology of "the democratic age." Democracy, in so far as it is a real political philosophy, and not a deliberately assumed mask for bourgeois oligarchy, is based upon the belief that reason is the main motive force of human action, and that men in the mass are, if properly educated, always prepared to accept programmes by reason of their justice, rationality, and wisdom. It is a captivating theory, so captivating that it dominated progressive political thought for nearly a century, and the only serious objection to it is that it is not true. Nor is it socialist, as the left wing understands socialism ; it is merely an abiding heritage of liberalism. Surely it is a commonplace to-day that, while reason may serve at times to light the path (otherwise life were indeed a tale told by an idiot, full of sound and fury, signifying nothing), the drive along

SOCIAL SOLIDARITY 87

that path comes preponderantly from the urge of the unconscious will. " Impulse," writes Bertrand Russell, " has more effect than conscious purpose in moulding men's lives." Bernard Shaw is fond of insisting that " we find reasons for what we want to do." A main part of the work of the Freudians, who are rapidly transmuting our knowledge of the human psyche, has been devoted to demonstrating the persistent sway of the unconscious. But of the Freudians or of Bergson we need not speak at length here, since we shall return to the matter in the chapter on " Creative Revolution." There we shall hope to show, if only in brief outline, that both Bergsonian indeterminism and Freudian determinism have important contributions to make to the modernised theory of revolutionary socialism. Suffice it here to challenge MacDonald's facile acceptance of liberal and democratic tradition. Those who expect, in the existing order, to persuade a competent majority that socialism is sweetly reasonable, to inspire with a conviction of sin the minority that has to be dispossessed so that it may relinquish without a struggle the privileges and powers deriving from the ownership of the means of production and the associated control of political power, are more hopelessly utopian than any writers of avowed utopian romances, and their proper dwelling-place is in the Cuckoo-Cloudland of the Greek comic dramatist. Such theories had a place in the days of Good Queen Victoria, but, like the name of Wettin, they have grown

38 CREATIVE REVOLUTION

somewhat musty of late, and belong to the era of pre-war psychology.

Our present task is mainly one of analysis, one of classification of divergent trends, and we cannot now undertake to elaborate the criticism of democracy. Of Fabianism, statism, and labourism, little more need be said. Fabianism is statism ; its method is not democratic but bureaucratic ; many of the earlier Fabians may have paid something more than lip-service to democracy, but the Fabianism that inspires the Labour Party is oligarchical and bureaucratic through and through, and any homage rendered to democracy is rendered with the tongue in the cheek. Still more hypocritical is the homage which, in times of stress, some of our great labour leaders pay to direct action ; such homage justifies a bitter cartoon published a few years ago by a reactionary comic paper. A " respectable " parliamentarian, labour member for Blank, is seen hastening after a crowd of workers on strike. One of his middle-class Westminster associates intervenes : " Good heavens, Smith, why on earth are you running after that disorderly mob ? "—" Don't stop me," replies the labour member ; " I must follow them ; I AM THEIR LEADER ! " Of such a type is the leadership of those who at long intervals are galvanised into activity by the pressure of the rank and file, and who devote the intervening periods to earning their salaries by maintaining their reputation for statesmanship.

Ramsay MacDonald, who shares with bourgeois

SOCIAL SOLIDARITY 39

politicians like Morley, Burns, and Trevelyan, the credit for resigning a comfortable post at the outset of the war, deserves more serious consideration. This advocate of social solidarity, this devotee of parliamentary democracy, is fond of vivid metaphors, which he uses with remarkable skill. We will give him one to consider. Democracy means "people's rule"; plutocracy means "rich man's rule"; ochlocracy means "mob rule." By *ochlos*, the mob, we denote the unthinking crowd, including the un-class-conscious proletariat. With all the issues of life set awry by the class struggle, the "people" is not a real entity at all, and "democracy" is a figment. Democracy, to the Marxist's vision at any rate, is but a blend of ochlocracy and plutocracy; of the rule of the mob and the rule of the rich. Now *ochlos* and *plutos* ride a tandem cycle; *ochlos* does the hard work on the rear seat while *plutos* controls the steering wheel and wins the prize. Such is our picture of social solidarity to-day, such our conception of contemporary democracy.

One word more as to the effect of past socialist propaganda. The revolution that is at hand will be a complex resultant of many causes. But in no small measure it will be the outcome of the workers' refusal to continue running the capitalist machine as a profit-making enterprise "owned" by the members of a dominant class. Only a small minority of those who thus refuse will have a clear conception of what they wish to achieve by their refusal, will have a reasoned

40 CREATIVE REVOLUTION

conviction guiding the attempt to pluck socialist order out of the chaotic break-up of capitalism. The others will have no more than an obscure feeling that the existing system is one wherein they are always, somehow or other, " bested by the boss," and an obscure desire for better things. To that extent they have become class-conscious. Their class-consciousness will reveal itself as a revolutionary mass psychology, and will culminate in the production of conditions amid which swiftly moving forces can give to minorities majority power. MacDonald himself foresees this eventuality as one of two alternative possibilities, for he writes (we ignore his preliminary flourishes about demagogues and charlatans, tricksters and cheapjacks) : " Labour troubles will become chronic, restlessness will defy reason, anarchy will spread, and social cohesion will be destroyed. Then also the duty of socialists will be clear. That will be the friction which causes the revolution, that will be the hindrance which makes ideas explosive. The socialists alone can then save the state, and a decisive act of commanding will will be required to do it. It may be a minority that will have to act, but in this process of creating revolutionary conditions, the majority will have been deprived of its authority, of its intelligence, of its defences, of justice. It will be weakened by fear, and will be made cowardly by its own sense of its criminality and unworthiness."

We would rather feel sure that in the supreme hour the ruling class (MacDonald does not really

SOCIAL SOLIDARITY 41

mean "the majority") will be weakened by something more potent than a sense of criminality and unworthiness, will be weakened by material facts, by an inability to depend on the men who have to fire the machine guns, to man the tanks and the submarines, to fly the aeroplanes, and to liberate the poison gas. Let that consideration pass and let us ask why labour troubles will become chronic, and all the rest of it. Quite apart from the causes MacDonald enumerates, high prices and so on, these things will be the fruit of socialist propaganda, which will have given definiteness of aim to an otherwise vague discontent, will have made revolution possible and inevitable where otherwise nothing would have resulted beyond sporadic revolts. A goodly part of that propaganda has been the street corner propaganda of the I.L.P. Now in so far as socialist propaganda has been truly effective, it has not—such is our contention, based on our reading of modern psychological science quite as much as on our adhesion to Marxist economics and sociology— been effective mainly because of rhetorical appeals to reason and justice, but mainly because it has, wittingly or unwittingly, pursued the tactic of the class struggle : because it has, designedly or undesignedly, aroused a revolutionary impulse among the mass of the workers to secure improved conditions of life and labour ; among a large number, to achieve self-government in industry ; and among the peculiarly intelligent minority, to throw off for ever the yoke of

CREATIVE REVOLUTION

capitalism, to abolish wage-slavery, and to make an end of ownership rule. If those who are animated with this revolutionary will, endeavour to achieve their ends through direct action, if they are convinced that to reach the land of Canaan they must take a short cut out of the parliamentary desert in which they have been wandering for forty years, it is not for would-be leaders to gainsay them. That is their vision, and they will follow it to the end, undismayed by the fact that many of those who have helped them thus far on the road now shrink back with horror from the contemplation of the forms which the final struggle is assuming. Marx and Engels, seventy years ago, had Pisgahsights of the promised land. To-day Lenin, Trotsky, and the Russian proletariat and poorer peasantry, occupy the outlying regions. Here, we shall not follow blindly in their footsteps, for in Britain, in France, in Italy, in Germany, in America, each proletariat has its own peculiar problems to face. But, broadly speaking, the left-wing socialists in all lands are agreed upon two points at least. They hold that parliament is outworn, and that the growing economic power of the workers must fashion new forms of political expression. And they are confident that the main impetus of advance must be the vital impetus of the class struggle.

CHAPTER THREE

SOCIALISM THROUGH THE CLASS STRUGGLE

The working class and the employing class have nothing in common. . . . Between these two classes a struggle must go on until the workers of the world, organised as a class, take possession of the earth and the machinery of production, and abolish the wage system.

PREAMBLE OF THE INDUSTRIAL WORKERS OF THE WORLD.

CHAPTER THREE

SOCIALISM THROUGH THE CLASS STRUGGLE

IN *Roads to Freedom*, Bertrand Russell passes a telling criticism on Marx. " Like the orthodox economists," he writes, " Marx imagined that men's opinions [? actions] are guided by a more or less enlightened view of economic self-interest, or rather of economic class-interest. A long experience of the workings of political democracy has shown that in this respect Disraeli and Bismarck were shrewder judges of human nature than either liberals or socialists." It is true that Marx, living in an age of hyper-rationalisation, was not wholly free from the intellectualist fallacy of believing man to be preeminently a rational animal. But the author of the materialist conception of history has more often been charged with underestimating than with overestimating the importance of reason as the driving force in social life. Eight years ago " Le Mouvement Socialiste " was discussing the affinities between Marx and Bergson, and the editor declared that it was mainly the " anti-intellectualism " of Bergson which had attracted his own attention. " Is not the realism of Marx and

46 CREATIVE REVOLUTION

Bergson," he asked, " hostile at bottom to every intellectualist doctrine ? " Herein we see foreshadowed the basis of the subsidiary canon in our classification of socialisms ; the recognition that socialists who believe that there already exists a working social solidarity, trust in general to intellectual persuasion, and hope to convince even the beneficiaries of capitalism that the claims of the workers are essentially " just " ; whereas the exponents of the class struggle, those to whom the class conflict seems a supreme tactical method as well as a descriptive fact, look for salvation to the urge of the revolutionary will, and base their hope of victory upon power rather than upon justice. Persons who hold such views will not be turned from their course by any sermonising about " the false god of the science of power." Power, they say, is misused by the exploiting class and the exploiting nationality for the purposes of exploitation. But power is essential to the exploited class and to the exploited nationality, to make good its enfranchisement from exploitation—at any rate during the initial stages and during the transition. Yet, as regards "reason," we must not throw the child out when we are emptying the bath. Class-war socialists believe that men are generally guided by economic class-interest when they are *aware* of it. The object of the working of bourgeois political and educational institutions is to prevent proletarians from becoming aware of the meaning of their proletarian status, to persuade them that they

THE CLASS STRUGGLE

are " citizens of the state." On the other hand, the object of such teaching as that contained in the *Preamble of the I.W.W.* (that " pernicious organisation," as A. G. Gardiner termed it not long ago in the " Daily News ") is to convince them that they are proletarians first, last, and all the time ; that the citizenship of the capitalist state is of value solely to the beneficiaries of capitalism ; and that there is no possible community of interest between a class that lives by ownership and a class that lives by labour.

Let us turn once more to consider the views of Bertrand Russell. We quote this time from an earlier work, *Principles of Social Reconstruction* : " In judging of an industrial system, whether the one under which we live or one proposed by reformers, there are four main tests which may be applied. We may consider whether the system secures (1) the maximum of production, or (2) justice in distribution, or (3) a tolerable existence for the producers, or (4) the greatest possible freedom and stimulus to vitality and progress." Capitalism, he goes on to say, aims essentially at maximum production, whereas socialism aims at justice in distribution and a tolerable existence for the producers. [Capitalism aims at maximum production for profit, not at maximum production for use, and herein lies one of its fundamental evils.] Some defenders of the present system contend, adds Bertrand Russell, " that technical progress is better promoted by private enterprise than it would be if industry were in the hands

48 CREATIVE REVOLUTION

of the state ; to this extent they recognise the fourth of the objects we have enumerated. But they recognise it only on the side of the capitalist, not on the side of the wage-earner. I believe that the fourth is much the most important of the objects to be aimed at, that the present system is fatal to it, and that orthodox [i.e. right-wing] socialism would prove equally fatal." On subsequent pages he underlines the main items of his own teaching. " I do not think that justice alone is a sufficient principle upon which to base an economic reconstruction. . . . The chief defect of the capitalist system is that work done for wages very seldom affords any outlet for the creative impulse. . . . This result is due to our industrial system, but it would not be avoided under state socialism. . . . In seeking a political theory which is to be useful at any given moment, what is wanted is not the invention of a Utopia, but the discovery of the best direction of movement. . . . Useful thought is that which indicates the right direction at the present time. . . . Men desire to enslave others more than they desire to be free themselves. . . . The supreme principle, both in politics and in private life, should be to promote all that is creative, and so to diminish the impulses and desires that centre round possession." In this volume and in *Roads to Freedom*, Russell goes on to develop the ideas which lead him to support the methods of social reconstruction advocated by the guild socialists. Before we touch lightly upon these, let us ask

THE CLASS STRUGGLE 49

what is meant by syndicalists, industrial unionists, guild socialists, and left-wingers generally, when they speak of " the abolition of the wage system." To this end we cannot do better than summarise the exposition given by G. D. H. Cole, one of the ablest advocates of guild socialism, in a chapter of his *Self-Government in Industry*. There are, says Cole, four distinguishing marks of the wage system: (1) by that system " labour " [he means " labour-power "] is abstracted from the labourer, so that the one can be bought and sold without the other ; (2) consequently, wages are paid to the wage-worker only when it is profitable to the capitalist to employ him ; (3) the wage-worker, in return for his wage, surrenders all control over the organisation of production ; (4) the wage-worker, in return for his wage, surrenders all claim upon the product of his labour.

It will be obvious from the foregoing summary that Cole regards the trouble of the wage-labourer as primarily one of status. In emerging from feudalism, men are grandiloquently said to have passed " from status to contract," but it is a familiar tenet of socialist criticism that this emancipation is, as far as the workers are concerned, mainly if not wholly illusory. We reaffirm the existence of the slave status when we speak of " wage-slavery " ; we do not use the term as a mere picturesque metaphor, or simply to stimulate the revolutionary will of the workers. During his " free " hours, the wage-worker has such limited freedoms as the

50 CREATIVE REVOLUTION

proletarian can command, the freedom of the public house, the picture palace, and the rack-rented tenement in which he dwells. Even during these "free" hours he is continually paying tribute in one way or another to rival forms of capitalist enterprise, much as the Chinese coolie in the Federated Malay States, after sweating throughout the day under a tropical sun, devotes the cool of the evening to getting rid of the greater part of his wages, which pass back into the clutches of the opium-farmer, the gambling-farmer, the brothel-keeper, and other protegees of British civilisation in the Far East. But during his working hours the proletarian toils for a master. His boasted freedom disappears, and in the factory or work-shop he finds scant opportunity for the exercise of the creative impulse. There are then, says Cole, four requisites which must be fulfilled before we can consider that the wage system has been abolished : (1) the worker must be recognised and paid as a human being, and not merely as the mortal tenement of so much labour-power for which an effective demand exists ; (2) consequently, he must be paid in employment and unemployment, in sickness and health alike ; (3) he must be empowered to control the organisation of production in common with his fellows ; (4) he must have a claim upon the product of his work, also exercised in co-operation with his fellows. By such changes the wage system could be abolished, even without complete communism.

THE CLASS STRUGGLE 51

In another eloquent passage in the same volume, Cole emphasises this question of status, and shows that to the class-war socialists of his school the primary need for the worker is not the securing of more material goods, but more liberty, and essentially, as Russell would phrase it, more scope for the exercise of the creative impulse. "What," Cole enquires, " is the fundamental evil in modern society which we should set out to abolish ? There are two answers to that question, and I am sure that very many well-meaning people would make the wrong one. They would answer POVERTY when they ought to answer SLAVERY. Face to face every day with the shameful contrasts of riches and destitution, high dividends and low wages, and painfully conscious of the futility of trying to adjust the balance by means of charity, private or public, they would answer unhesitatingly that they stand for the abolition of poverty. Well and good ! On that issue every socialist is with them. But their answer to my question is none the less wrong. Poverty is the symptom : slavery the disease. The extremes of riches and destitution follow inevitably upon the extremes of licence and bondage. The many are not enslaved because they are poor, they are poor because they are enslaved. Yet socialists have all too often fixed their eyes upon the material misery of the poor without realising that it rests upon the spiritual degradation of the slave."

It would probably be an error to assert that

52 CREATIVE REVOLUTION

all the socialisms which must be denoted " class-war socialisms " have been consciously animated by a desire to escape from slavery rather than to put an end to poverty. The bourgeois intellectual, however keen his socialist sympathies, is apt to underestimate the value of " mere material goods." Often enough he fails to understand how transcendent the importance of a little more food, of somewhat warmer clothing, of a roomier dwelling, and above all of a little more leisure, is to those whose supply of these goods has ever been measured out with a niggard hand. Yet it is impossible to contemplate the various left-wing movements of the last few years, to study the literature of the I.W.W., syndicalism, and the one-big-union movement, without realising that these literatures are animated by the spirit of revolt against slavery. Still more do we feel this when we study the most remarkable of all modern working-class movements, or the movement which was the most remarkable prior to the occurrence of the bolshevik revolution, the British movement for independent working-class education. When we read the files of the " Plebs Magazine " from the day of the revolt at Ruskin College down to our own time, when we study the controversy between the Plebs League and the Workers' Educational Association, we breathe the very atmosphere of the class war, and we realise that here we have come into contact with a fully conscious revolt against industrial slavery. " The syndicalists " writes Bertrand Russell,

THE CLASS STRUGGLE 53

"have revived the quest for liberty, which was growing somewhat dimmed under the regime of parliamentary socialism, and they have reminded men that what our modern society needs is not a little tinkering here and there, nor the kind of minor readjustments to which the existing holders of power may readily consent, but a fundamental reconstruction, a sweeping away of all the sources of oppression, a liberation of men's constructive energies, and a wholly new way of conceiving and regulating production and economic relations."

Bertrand Russell, despite the keenness of his sympathies and the comprehensiveness of his intelligence, is a trifle academic. He knows well enough that the earlier syndicalist movement, though splendidly rebellious, was lacking in the constructive side. There was to be increasing vigour in the promotion of the class war, culminating in the general strike, and then —oh, well, then the workers, organised as a class, would take possession of the earth and the machinery of production, and would abolish the wage system. But just how the workers would do these things was not made particularly plain in the syndicalist system of thought, while any attempt to attain to clarity of vision was apt to be discouraged by the evangelists of the new creed. "You talk utopia," they were wont to say. True, Pataud and Pouget, in their well-known book *Syndicalism and the Cooperative Commonwealth*, attempted an outline sketch of revolutionary reconstruction ; and

54   CREATIVE REVOLUTION

the industrial unionists of America had done much before the war to work out the constructive side of their theories. But the pictures are based more on fancy than on induction, and they fail to grip the imagination. It is natural that Russell should perceive the gap in the syndicalist method ; it is natural that, himself a typical intellectual of aristocratic culture, he should welcome the constructive suggestions of guild socialism, the theory which a group of able young bourgeois intellectuals (the heirs in this generation of the energy which went to the making of Fabianism thirty-five years ago) have for some time been endeavouring to impose upon the working-class movement in this country. Had Russell been more in touch with the real working-class movement, he would have known that everywhere, and preeminently in Britain, that movement is throwing up its own intellectuals ; that syndicalism has a proletarian intellectual side as well as a semi-bourgeois intellectual side ; that the Plebs League and the Labour Colleges are the working-class counterblast to the middle-class National Guilds League and the Workers' Educational Association ; and that the proletarian movement, not the semi-bourgeois movement, is the true inheritor of the liberty-ensuing energies of syndicalism. He would have known further that on the industrial side, with constructive political possibilities of the widest scope, there has now developed the shop stewards' and workers' committees' movement, a spontaneous British development, and

THE CLASS STRUGGLE 55

simultaneously the British counterpart of the soviet evolution and revolution in bolshevist Russia.

To the shop stewards' and workers' committees we shall devote the next chapter. Here we are merely trying to analyse the development of socialist theory before the bolshevist revolution, and we wish to give to the work of the Plebs League and the Labour Colleges its proper place in the picture. This work represents a deliberate endeavour to incorporate into working-class education the doctrine and the tactic of the class struggle. The League and the Colleges originated, as we have said, out of a revolt against the social solidarity trend of Ruskin College and the Workers' Educational Association, against the idea that as far as an industrial worker needs " higher education," the function of that education must be to " make him at once a more efficient servant of his own society and a more potent influence upon the side of industrial peace . . . that he may be a good citizen and play a reasonable part in the world " ; against the notion, propagated in a textbook of industrial history by a member of Ruskin College staff, that " fortunately [shades of Admiral Bacon !] the antagonism between the two sets of forces is more apparent than real." The Central Labour College was established to educate the workers in the interests of the workers ; it was founded and financed by the South Wales Miners and the Amalgamated Society of Railway Servants. It represented,

56 CREATIVE REVOLUTION

and continues to represent, the educational side of the syndicalist spirit. The Plebs League (we quote from a pamphlet issued in 1917 entitled *What does Education mean to the Workers?*) "seeks to further the interests of Independent Working-Class Education as a PARTIZAN effort to improve the position of labour in the present, ultimately assisting in the abolition of wage slavery." Education, it declares, "is not an end in itself, but a means to an end," and the end is to promote the victory of the labour movement. This movement "has its basis in the antagonism of interests existing between capital and labour. . . . The education with which it is concerned must be based on a recognition of this same antagonism." And the motto of the League is " I can promise to be candid but not impartial." No compromise here! We have the educational aspect of the preamble of the I.W.W. The movement glows with revolutionary fire. It is a glorious embodiment of the vital impetus. It is, as the " Times " had reluctantly to admit in a series of articles published in the summer of 1917, the very ferment of revolution!

Our attempt to classify the two trends of the contemporary socialist movement, the trends that were obvious to all the world prior to the summer of 1917, draws to a close. We have endeavoured to be "candid" in our representation of the theories of the social solidarians, but would not for a moment claim that we have been " impartial." For we, too, are

THE CLASS STRUGGLE 57

" Plebeians," and we are of opinion that the socialist Laodiceans are more dangerous to the movement than the most outspoken among our foes. Of all Marx's contributions to socialist thought, the greatest in our estimation, and the one most assuredly confirmed by the march of events, was his proclamation of the tactic of the class struggle. This theory of the class struggle, as a means for realising socialism, the whole of socialism, and nothing but socialism, here and now, is the supreme dread of the master class. Class-war socialism is the only sort of socialism which they do dread. That is why they term it " bolshevism," in contradistinction to " moderate " or " sane " socialism—and that is one of the reasons why we of the left wing delight to inscribe bolshevism on our standard.

Before the war it was difficult to get an average British proletarian audience to listen to talk of the class struggle. During the more active stages of the war it was not easy to talk about the class struggle without enjoying the hospitalities of prison ! But more than four years' experience of war and a year's experience of the desolation to which our imperialist rulers have given the name of peace, have wrought a miracle, so that even the British worker is beginning to realise his proletarian status. British tanks in George Square to terrorise the Clyde workers, British troops to break the power of a Belfast soviet—these were portents which it needed no Joseph to interpret. The police strike, the railway strike, the cessation

58 CREATIVE REVOLUTION

of the unemployment " dole " at the outset of a hard winter contemporaneously with a dole of an additional fifteen million sterling to Denikin, have been instructive phenomena during the first year of the " new world " that has issued from the war for liberty. The day is coming, and coming speedily, when the capitalist Humpty Dumpty will be thrown from the wall upon which he is seated, and not all the king's horses and all the king's men, aided by all the tame labour battalions commanded by the Kerenskis and the Vanderveldes, by the Noskes and the Scheidemanns, by the Thomases and the Hendersons, will ever set Humpty Dumpty up again. The tame labour battalions are dwindling, and the " wild men " are becoming increasingly numerous. Nor are the army and navy and the air force immune to the ferment of revolution ; and perhaps when the hour strikes some of the " king's " horses and the " king's " men will be fighting on the side of the revolution. There is considerable doubt whether the aforesaid tanks in George Square were anything more than ornamental, whether the guns would have gone off at the word of command. We do not build too much on the possibilities of " corrupting " the armed forces of the crown. We remember that the sailors, the soldiers, and the airmen (or at any rate the air-mechanics) are but workers in uniform, but we know the potent influence of military discipline. There are other methods for ensuring the victory of the workers when the decisive moment comes, and the main

THE CLASS STRUGGLE

point is that a revolutionary mass psychology is spreading, for the workers have begun to see. In Ukrainian folk-lore we read of a being known as the Vii [Vēē], whose aspect is that of an old man with enormous pendent eyelids reaching to the very ground. The Vii, therefore, can see nothing; but if a strong man lift up its eyelids with a pitchfork, then nothing is hidden from its terrible gaze. With a mere glance the Vii can destroy everything that stands in its way, can pulverise towns and villages. In Russia the Vii has been seeing clearly since November, 1917. In Britain, the war and the peace are the prongs of the pitchfork, and the left-wing socialists are the strong man who is making the workers see. There are enough of them to do this yeoman's service. Some of them may be imprisoned, some of them may be struck down; but others will arise to continue the work. The hour is at hand. "The knell of capitalist property sounds; the expropriators are expropriated." The call to arms has sounded! Close ranks the foe to face! The Workers' International shall be the human race! March onward O army of the toilers! STRAIGHT TO THE GOAL!

CHAPTER FOUR

THE SHOP STEWARDS' MOVEMENT

Away with wreckage of past nations !
Enslavéd crowd, rise at the call !
The world shall change from its foundations ;
We that are nothing, shall be all.

THE INTERNATIONAL.

To obtain an ever-increasing control of workshop conditions, the regulation of the terms upon which the workers shall be employed, the organisation of the workers upon a class basis to prosecute the interests of the working class until the triumph of the workers is assured.

OBJECTS OF THE NATIONAL SHOP STEWARDS'
AND WORKERS' COMMITTEES.

CHAPTER FOUR

THE SHOP STEWARDS' MOVEMENT

ADOPTING Masaryk's phraseology, we may say that, broadly speaking, the political history of the western world can be summarised as a passage from theocratic aristocracy to bourgeois or capitalist democracy. We are now in the throes of transition to a new phase, and the change is likely to be accomplished in decades instead of centuries, in years instead of decades. The transition this time is from capitalist democracy to communist ergatocracy. Apart from the inelegance of the term, we could not properly speak of the new order as " communist dictatorship of the proletariat." The dictatorship is no more than a transient and necessary evil, the revolutionary reversal of the veiled oligarchy of the bourgeoisie, and we shall pass, speedily it may be hoped, through dictatorship to ergatocracy.

Capitalism is doomed. Behind its solid-seeming front the entire structure is crumbling to ruin. The alternative that faces us is not the alternative between capitalism and socialism, but the alternative between socialism and chaos. It grows increasingly clear that socialism will

64 CREATIVE REVOLUTION

never be secured through parliamentary democracy, that our goal can be attained only through communist ergatocracy. Parliament, whatever it may have been in its origins, has become essentially an instrument for the maintenance and diffusion of capitalist democracy ; a democracy which boasts of giving equal rights to such folk as Northcliffe and Rockefeller, and is therefore ruled by such folk as Northcliffe and Rockefeller, and by the Lloyd Georges and the Wilsons who are their tools ; a democracy whose very thoughts are suggested by the press, the school, and the cinema controlled by the capitalist oligarchs. We shall court failure should we attempt to put our new ergatocratic wine into the old parliamentary bottles. Clear-sighted revolutionists recognise that parliament is obsolete, and must be thrown on the scrap-heap. Those who realise that the parliamentary machine is out-of-date must show their colours. It is sheer waste of time for us to trouble ourselves over parliamentary paraphernalia, to interest ourselves in elections to the gas-factory at Westminster, to lobby labour members, to participate in delegations to cabinet ministers. We have to devote ourselves to the fashioning of the new tool. We must concentrate our energies upon organising and educating our fellow-workers, so that when the favourable moment comes there may be an adequate revolutionary minority able to avail itself of the new instrument, and a mass psychology which may at least not be hostile to its employment.

THE SHOP STEWARDS' MOVEMENT 65

And the new instrument, the workers' committee or soviet, will express working-class social organisation far more effectively than parliament ever expressed bourgeois social organisation, for it is inspired with the awakened consciousness characteristic of our epoch. Its use involves the frank recognition that industry, the mechanism of production, is the driving force of contemporary social life.

The idea of communist ergatocracy is no mere theory imposed upon the working-class movement from above by a group of bourgeois intellectuals. The ergatocratic trend is the spontaneous outcome of the economic, social, and political changes going on under our very eyes. We see analogous developments along these lines in every land where the economic conditions are ripe. The quickened pulse of war has but accelerated a transformation which was already in progress before the war, and of which the syndicalist movement was an early and inchoate expression. As a sequel of the war, we see ergatocracy triumphant in Russia, revolting against the state socialism of Noske, flashing gloriously for a space in Hungary, and struggling towards fruition in our own land. The shop stewards' movement and the establishment of workers' committees are the British counterpart of the Russian soviet organisation; they are the British attempt to secure for the workers effective control of working conditions, and, incidentally, to bring about the revolution which socialists have for many decades been

66   CREATIVE REVOLUTION

vainly trying to achieve with the effete weapon of parliamentary democracy.

The ergatocratic movement is spontaneous and world-wide, and bodies similar to the workers' committees are springing to life in every land. France has its *délégués de l'atelier*; Germany has its *Werkstättenvertrauensmänner*; these exactly correspond to our own shop stewards. In the United States, the marvellous growth of the I.W.W. during the war took place on shop-steward lines, and substantially the most successful I.W.W. locals, those that have organised the lumbermen, the agricultural workers, etc., are, like our own shop committees, based upon working units; they aim at a class organisation which shall secure self-government in industry, and therewith abolish wage-slavery and overthrow capitalism and ownership rule. The impetus to the soviet movement in Turkestan and in the furthest east has doubtless come from soviet Russia. But in the main the " soviet " development, the ergatocratic trend, is a universal blossoming. In the most comprehensive sense of the term, the " bolshevik " movement is the joint outcome of new economic conditions cooperating with Marxist criticism and with Marxist conceptions of social reconstruction.

Almost simultaneously with the inauguration of the Clyde Workers' Committee as the local expression, under Marxist auspices, of the idea of the control of industry by workers with an ulterior revolutionary aim, was held the Zimmer-

THE SHOP STEWARDS' MOVEMENT 67

wald conference as an international expression, once more under Marxist auspices, of the replica of the same idea and as a formulation of the new political synthesis which was to translate from the realm of phrase-making into the world of fact the famous slogan of the *Communist Manifesto*, " Workers of the World Unite ! " This war, said the Zimmerwaldians, is not *our* war. Our war, the only war that matters, is the class war, which we shall wage relentlessly, and quite independently of the wishes of capitalist oligarchs organised in rival groups of allied " nationalities." The bolshevik revolution in Russia, though ostensibly led by prominent Zimmerwaldian intellectuals, was in truth the logical outcome of a movement which had been in progress among the revolutionary workers of Russia for ten years before the war, and was based upon the soviet method of organisation. Now the soviet is a synthesis of the two aspects, industrial and political, of the latter-day revolutionary working-class movement. It is a workers' committee assuming control of the political machine, and ignoring the sounding brass and tinkling cymbal of parliamentary democracy.

The shop stewards' movement aims primarily at perfecting the machinery of industrial unionism, and at securing the control of industry by the workers through workshop control. But the Marxists, who are the leading spirits among the shop stewards, know that the movement is before all revolutionary ; that in Britain, as in

68 CREATIVE REVOLUTION

Russia, it will once and for ever abolish the rule of those who live by ownership, and will substitute for that dominion the rule, or rather the administration, of those who live by labour ; that it will replace bourgeois democracy by communist ergatocracy. And though, by a confusion of terms which till a year ago was perhaps pardonable, many of those in the van of the movement continue to talk of their method as " anti-political " when they merely mean "anti-parliamentarian," the more clear-sighted apostles of the shop stewards' movement recognise that, that movement, besides being economic, social and educative, is likewise and preeminently political. Convinced as they are that economic power is the basis of political power, they are equally convinced that the shop stewards' movement is the germ of the means whereby the growing economic power of the workers will secure political expression. The Scottish Workers' Committees have just issued the first of a series of pamphlets which are to deal with the philosophy, the strategy, and the tactics of the " unofficial movement." Pamphlet No. 1, by William Gallacher and J. R. Campbell, is entitled *Direct Action*. We cull the following pregnant sentences : " The workers have to create organisations to counter the state organisation of capitalism. . . . The joint industrial and social committee would be the nucleus of working-class political power. As the industrial and social organisation grows strong enough it will be forced to fight the capitalist state, . . . not to

THE SHOP STEWARDS' MOVEMENT 69

take possession of it, but to smash it. The joint social and industrial committee would then have to assume many of the functions of the state during a period of transition."

The slave-holding system, the feudal system, the city patriciates of the days of guild production, and finally the capitalist system in its various phases down to the most recent developments of financial capital and state capitalism—all have been different varieties of ownership rule, and all have found their political expression in different varieties of class state. The revolutions whereby a later phase of proprietorship has been substituted for an earlier have been far less vital than the revolution now in progress wherein ownership rule will yield place to ergatocracy. This is the revolution in which the working class, rising at length to power, will permanently abolish class. This is the revolution in which the proletariat will fulfil its historic mission by realising communist ergatocracy, just as the bourgeoisie fulfilled its historic mission by realising capitalist democracy. Since the days when, with the growth of what for three-quarters of a century has been known as the socialist movement, the function of the modern working class as a revolutionary force began to be understood, three main methods of advance have been simultaneously or successively essayed : trade unionism (old style) ; cooperation ; and labourism, or the attempt to organise the battalions of labour on the parliamentary battlefield, the attempt to secure the

70   CREATIVE REVOLUTION

triumph of the proletariat by wresting from the
bourgeoisie its own finished instrument of parliamentary democracy. It is needless, to-day, to
recapitulate the reasons for the failure of craft
unionism, which was revolutionary in its origins,
but which, as the years have rolled by, has been
ever more effectively " nobbled " in the interests
of the master class. Productive cooperation is
a proved impracticability so long as capitalism
is dominant ; so long as the capitalists control
the labour market, the produce market, and the
money market ; and so long as bourgeois ideology rules the world. Distributive cooperation,
too, still owes much of its strength to bourgeois
ideology, and to the dividend-hunting spirit
which continues to animate large sections of
the workers. Though not without its advantages
in certain respects, distributive cooperation is
as little likely to be the main instrument in the
revolution as a brigade of peashooters would be
to capture a maxim gun position. Parliamentary
democracy may be left to those socialists whose
robust faith in its efficiency still survives, and
to their labourist associates (titled and untitled,
decorated and undecorated, in office or discharged from office). No convinced ergatocrat
will wish to stake his money on a dead horse.
For new times, new methods. The fundamental
issue may be summed up in a single sentence.
The shop stewards' and workers' committees'
movement is the means by which the proletariat
will fulfil its historic mission ; in retrospect,
the shop stewards' movement will be recognised

THE SHOP STEWARDS' MOVEMENT 71

as the instrument of the twentieth century revolution, the revolution which inaugurated ergatocracy.

It is not suggested that the shop stewards and their supporters, all or most, are to-day consciously inspired by such an aim. Were they so inspired, communist ergatocracy in Great Britain would be a year or two nearer than it is. The immediate goal of the movement is to secure the control of industry by the workers through organisation in the workshop. The unit of organisation is the workshop committee, and the stewards who form this committee are elected by the workers in the various departments regardless of craft or sex. As with the soviet system in Russia, the organisation of the "unofficial movement" proceeds by the election of delegates to plant committees, from these to local or district committees, and from these to a national organisation, like the All-Russian soviet. The workers' committees originated under war stresses in the engineering trade, perhaps the most important industry in wartime. As the movement spreads to other industries, modifications are needed, and these are being worked out in accordance with the fundamental characteristics of each industry—as by the South Wales Socialist Society in their *Plan for the Democratic Control of the Mining Industry*, a recent successor to the famous pamphlet *The Miners' Next Step*. But in each industry the unit of organisation remains the working group, and in each the stress is laid,

72 CREATIVE REVOLUTION

not as in the old trade unionism upon craft, nor even as in industrial unionism upon industry, but above all upon CLASS. It is by class-conscious organisations able to carry on production that the workers can secure the control of industry, expropriate the " owners," and bring about the social revolution.

The point on which we have to insist in summarising the philosophy of the new development, is that the economic revolution known as the attainment of self-government in industry will inevitably involve the social revolution in its entirety—for capitalism is maintained by the rule of the owners in factory and workshop no less than in the state. The shop stewards' movement is an expression of the revolutionary will of the workers, and is one of the means by which that revolutionary will is rapidly creating a revolutionary situation. The downfall of capitalism will not result merely from the perplexities of post-war capitalist finance, nor will it be due exclusively to the increasing difficulty of disposing abroad of that surplus which is indispensable to capitalist production. The imminence of the revolutionary situation is in large part the outcome of the vital impulses of the bulk of the workers, who even in such a land as our own, where comparative prosperity has prevailed throughout the war, are showing greater and greater unwillingness to continue running the productive machine in the interest of a ruling class. But when that unwillingness culminates in a revolutionary situation, the

THE SHOP STEWARDS' MOVEMENT 73

workers, if they are not to starve, will have to take control of the machinery of production in order to run it in their own interest and that of the community. Nay, more. Unless the workers' committees, seizing control of industry, are fully prepared, not merely to maintain and more than maintain production, but further to assume and to discharge with enhanced efficiency and in the workers' interest the social, educative, and political functions now discharged (however inefficiently from the workers' point of view) by the various organs of the capitalist state—unless they are desirous of doing these things and competent to do these things, chaos will ensue ; or the capitalist state will remain in being, and the control of industry by the workers' committees will prove to have been nothing more than a breath on the face of the waters. The workers cannot fulfil their historic mission until the time is ripe ; and whether the time is or is not ripe we shall learn, as far as this country is concerned, by the manner in which, in the immediate future, the more active protagonists in the shop stewards' movement comport themselves in view of the needs of the hour.

The next few months are likely to show whether a revolutionary vital impetus really animates a sufficient section of the British workers, or whether the lower-middle-class mentality is still dominant even among the wage earners of this preeminently middle-class land. Apt, in this connection, are the words of Lenin in *The Soviets at Work* : " In a country

74 CREATIVE REVOLUTION

where the petty bourgeois population is vastly predominant in comparison with the purely proletarian, the difference between the proletarian and the petty bourgeois revolutionist will inevitably appear, and from time to time very sharply. The petty bourgeois revolutionist . . . wavers at every turn of events, . . . hesitating between confidence . . . and fits of despair. . . . Socialism cannot be built on such foundations. . . . We need the regular march of the iron battalions of the proletariat." Agreed, tavarish, agreed ; but these same iron battalions must know whither they are marching, and how best to advance along the road. We have no Lenin here, nor need of one. Russian conditions are peculiar, and perchance an ex-aristocratic intellectual such as yourself, an ex-bourgeois intellectual such as Trotsky, may have been indispensable factors in the bolshevik revolution. Here the working-class movement is fashioning its own intellectuals in the labour colleges and the Marxist classes ; is turning them out by hundreds at a time. Such men and women have no parliamentary ambitions, no taste for the honeyed sweets of trade-union officialdom. Except for those who become teachers in the colleges or join the staffs of the new revolutionary papers, they remain workers in the industrial field, and there they can best carry on the campaign which is their labour of love. There, in the mill, in the workshop, in the mine, they can diffuse the revolutionary virus, deadly to our enemies, but the very breath of life to

THE SHOP STEWARDS' MOVEMENT 75

ourselves. True, indeed, is what Lenin said to Ransome: "England may seem to you untouched, but the microbe is already there."

Yes, the microbe is already here! The shop stewards' movement is a manifestation of creative evolution. Ere long, we hope, it will enter the revolutionary phase, and will become one of the most potent instruments of creative revolution. But for the nonce it remains in the evolutionary stage and must concentrate its energies upon the perfectionment of organisation. Here we encounter one of the problems of the moment. What should be the attitude of the revolutionary shop steward, of the communist ergatocrat, of the sovietist, towards certain contemporary institutions, and notably towards the representative institutions of bourgeois democracy, towards distributive cooperation, and towards extant trade unionism?

The question of abstentionism from parliamentary and municipal struggles will be considered in the tenth chapter. The trade unions and the cooperatives are on an entirely different footing from parliament and the other institutions of bourgeois democracy. Despite their many and glaring defects, they originated as organs of the class struggle, and can be usefully coordinated for participation in that struggle. The management of the cooperatives is still impregnated with bourgeois ideology, and in the fight between the Amalgamated Union of Cooperative Employees and the Cooperative Wholesale Society we find the directors of the

76 CREATIVE REVOLUTION

cooperative movement displaying the mentality of the profit-making master class. The sovietist will certainly not desire to sweep away the cooperatives. In fact, he will himself be a cooperator. But he has more important work in hand than to participate, at this juncture, in the growth of distributive cooperation. He hopes, when the revolution comes, that cooperative institutions will here, as in Russia, prove of considerable service to the workers. For the time being, the bourgeois distributive services will be paralysed ; and when the distributive machinery of modern society gets to work again, it will have to be reorganised largely on cooperative lines. Meanwhile the sovietist's business is to " ergatocratise " the cooperatives, to promote the spread of shop stewardism among the cooperative employees, so that efficient workers' committees, affiliated to the National Shop Stewards' and Workers' Committees, may be organised in every cooperative department throughout the land, ready, when the time is ripe, to carry on distribution in the interest of the revolutionary workers.

Similarly reconstructive, at once critical and sympathetic, must be the attitude of the sovietist towards trade unionism. In some of the workers' committees the idea has been mooted that the old trade unions are as effete as parliament, and are as little likely as parliament to promote the real interests of the class-conscious proletariat. Those who take this view would like to see the whole obsolete machinery scrapped, and they

THE SHOP STEWARDS' MOVEMENT 77

contend that at any rate trade unionism can be contemptuously ignored. But there are three strong objections to this view.

In the first place the trade unions, ineffective as they have proved from the outlook of the ardent revolutionist, have none the less been potent instruments of creative evolution. Throughout the whole century of their existence they have been continuously operative in maintaining the workers' standard of life, and have, for all their failings, been valuable organs of education as well as defence. Even were the workers' committees destined wholly to supersede trade unions, the time has not yet come for abandoning the trade union trenches.

In the second place we have to consider the psychology of the less instructed among the organised workers. These have at least got one fruitful idea into their heads, and that is the idea of organisation for defence against the rapacity of the employing class. The average trade unionist will listen in the workshop to one who points out that his trade union has conspicuous defects as a fighting organism ; that craft unionism is a back number, and that industrial unionism among the workers is requisite to face the powers of large-scale industrial capital ; that the one-big-union would perhaps be best of all. He will attend with interest and usually with sympathy to the suggestion that for the needs of the hour, to cope with the changed conditions of modern industrial

78　CREATIVE REVOLUTION

life, he must supplement trade unionism, industrial unionism, one-big-unionism, by organisations of the new type, by shop stewards' and workers' committees or soviets. But one who opens the campaign for sovietism by telling his workmates that the workers' committees are not to supplement but to replace the trade unions is likely to be informed in the homely vernacular that he is a " bloody blackleg," and is certain to find that he is casting his seed upon barren ground.

Last of all, it is improbable that trade unionism is destined to be wholly superseded. Even craft unionism of the narrower sort may find a place in the future commonwealth. It seems probable that the workers in the various industries will remain organised on industrial unionist lines. How far creative evolution will work out a type of organisation resembling, on the industrial side, that sketched by the theorists of guild socialism, need not concern us. But at any rate a long time is likely to elapse before such bodies of workers as the miners and the railway men cease to feel the need for a specific industrial organisation to represent their own particular interests. On the other hand, in the case of industries of this type, perforce centralised, there must, as far as can be foreseen, exist a centralised body peculiar to each industry, to deal on a national scale with questions of production and distribution. The workers' committees in such industries will have to see to it that there is no bureaucratic tyranny, no

THE SHOP STEWARDS' MOVEMENT 79

abuse of power, on the part of the union, or on the part of what (until it has "died out") we may continue to call the state. But the industrial union is likely to survive throughout the period of transition. It is futile, therefore, to talk of scrapping the trade unions which will grow into these great corporations of the future. This is no matter of pure theory. In Russia, just as the cooperatives have not merely survived but have played, and continue to play, a role of supreme importance, so also, after the revolution, will there be abundant scope for the activities of what, in the new Russia, are termed " professional unions."

CHAPTER FIVE

**HISTORICAL
SIGNIFICANCE
OF THE
GREAT
WAR**

And I looked, and behold a pale horse : and his name that
sat on him was Death, and Hell followed with him.   And power
was given unto them over the fourth part of the earth, to kill
with sword and with hunger, and with death, and with the
beasts of the earth.

APOCALYPSE OF JOHN.

Last as first the question rings
Of the Will's long travailings ;
Why the All-mover,
Why the All-prover
Ever urges on and measures out the droning tune of Things.

Hearing dumbly
As we deem,
Moulding numbly
As in dream,
Apprehending not how fare the sentient subjects of Its scheme.

.   .   .   .

But a stirring thrills the air
Like to sounds of joyance there
That the rages
Of the ages
Shall be cancelled, and deliverance offered from the darts that
were,
Consciousness the Will informing, till It fashion all things fair !

THOMAS HARDY.

CHAPTER FIVE

HISTORICAL SIGNIFICANCE OF THE GREAT WAR

BRIEFLY summarised, our conception of the meaning of the years 1914 to 1919 may be read by a quickened imagination from the extracts that head this chapter. The war is not to be regarded as a conflict of rival idealisms culminating in the victory of the more exalted of the twain; it is not, as has been conceived on Bergsonian lines, a victory of the vital impetus (France and her allies) effecting an irresistible upward progress in defiance of the downward drift of lifeless matter (Germany and her associates); it has not been, to quote Benjamin Kidd's phrasing of the same idea, " the struggle of the comparatively small class who have held military power in modern Germany against the soul of the world "; it is not to ᴸe looked upon as the outcome of a divine purpose using on a stupendous scale and for the ends of progress the terrible winnowing fan of slaughter. Should we succumb to the almost universal inclination towards reading our own mental characteristics into the universe, we may say, as Hardy says in *The Dynasts* and elsewhere, that we see Impulse without Purpose,

84   CREATIVE REVOLUTION

that the Immanent Will has been working, as ever, in its unweeting way. Similar catastrophes have happened often before in human history, though but twice or thrice on a scale anything like so gigantic. We think, first of all, of the long centuries marked by the invasion of the barbarian hordes, the collapse of Roman civilisation, the replacement of Paganism by Christianity, and the transformation of a slave system of production into the systems typical of the middle ages. We think, next, of the overthrow of the medieval systems and the inauguration of the era of capitalist production. Likewise long drawn out, this phase interlaces at the ends with the antecedent and subsequent phases. Russian serfdom, for instance, had in it a strong kinship with the chattel slavery of the classical age, while the most finished form of chattel slavery was the capitalist-tinged slavery in the southern states of the Union during the years preceding the civil war. But, on the whole, the period from about 1450 to the days of the French revolution may be looked upon as the second great period of transition, when the foundations of the modern bourgeois world were being laid upon the ruins of feudalism and the guild system. The most disastrous interludes of conflict during this era were the wars of religion and the Napoleonic wars. The latest age of transition (the last, we may hope, to be distinguished by the blind surrender of man to the unweeting will, or to the impulses of gods who kill us for their sport) is that through which we are now

SIGNIFICANCE OF THE GREAT WAR 85

living. The Great War marks the nadir of capitalism, following swiftly upon its zenith, upon the glorious era of capitalist imperialism. And Consciousness, the Will informing, though it may not fashion all things fair, will yet succeed in making human social progress definitely aware of its own aims, and at least less grisly than what Winwood Reade has poignantly termed the martyrdom of man. The war of 1914–18 is the close of the long agony of unconscious drift at the mercy of blind economic and social forces; the Russian revolution of November, 1917, is the opening act in the great drama of purposive creative revolution.

But here we are chiefly concerned with the causes of the war and with its opening phases; the next chapter will be devoted to the lessons of the Russian revolution. Left-wing socialists are substantially agreed in their interpretation of the war. It seems to them to be a phenomenon parallel with the wars that raged during the eras referred to in the previous paragraph. The barbarian invasions, the outcome presumably of the pressure of population upon the means of subsistence, and perhaps the sequel of the secular drying-up of vast areas in Central Asia, were rather the final determinant than the essential cause of the break-up of slave-holding Roman imperialism. That system collapsed from its own inherent economic defects. Similarly with the wars of religion. The ideological causes that appeared on the surface were but a mask for underlying economic causes which

96 CREATIVE REVOLUTION

led to the disintegration of the international synthesis of Catholic Europe, to the break-up of feudalism, and to the gradual inauguration of the bourgeois era. So, too, the great revolution in France was not primarily the outcome of Rousseau's social theories or of the humanitarian enthusiasm of the encyclopedists; it originated in the financial collapse of the imperialist system bequeathed by the *grand monarque* to his descendants and successors. The Napoleonic wars were not solely conditioned by the dynastic ambitions of a megalomaniac; they were part of the perturbations consequent upon the close of one system and the inception of another. Such is the Marxist reading of the main outlines of European history. Be that interpretation right or be it wrong, the "materialist conception" throws a new and interesting light on happenings which seem far more obscure when we contemplate them with no better elucidation than that of ordinary historians. When we come to contemporary events, the Marxist reading is the only one which makes history intelligible. Before the war, the coming struggle was plainly foreshadowed as a practically inevitable outcome of capitalist imperialist rivalries. When the crash came, whilst the right-wing socialists and revisionists lapsed into the delirium of patriotism, and whilst the Independent Labour Party and similar bodies adopted a compromise attitude or wandered off into the desert of Tolstoyan pacifism, the revolutionary socialists of the left wing, with few

SIGNIFICANCE OF THE GREAT WAR 87

exceptions, rallied to the view which has been expressed by Trotsky in a trenchant formula: "the war of 1914 is the most colossal breakdown in history of a system destroyed by its own inherent contradictions."

A word in passing concerning our attitude towards those from whom we have been severed by the touchstone of war. We deprecate the tendency to lapse into abusive phraseology in relation to men and women who have been comrades-in-arms in less difficult and less strenuous times. Just as no reconciliation is possible between the outlook of Lenin and Trotsky on the one hand, and of Kautsky and Fritz Adler on the other; so in this country there can be no community of views between left-wingers and those who, throughout the war, taking the name of socialism in vain, supported one or other group of competing imperialists. But the writer, the thinker, the revolutionist to whom (without permission) we have dedicated this little book, errs, in our judgment, when he applies the harsh term "renegade" to such men as Plehanoff and Kautsky. We would withhold this label even from those who, during the war, obtained "honour" and emolument in the service of the capitalist government. These men are not renegades. They have not denied the movement; they have not turned their backs on the movement; but the movement has passed on to new conquests, leaving them, forlorn voluntary outcasts, marooned on desolate beaches.

88 CREATIVE REVOLUTION

The war, then, is the most colossal breakdown in history of an economic system destroyed by its own inherent contradictions. But it is more. It is an accelerator through whose operation the final phases of capitalist development and capitalist deadlock have been enormously compressed. And it is a revealer whereby the socialist consciousness of mankind, or rather of the class whose historic mission it is to overthrow capitalism and to inaugurate the new era of communist ergatocracy, has been intensified. At last, in sober truth, a stirring thrills the air, for man is about to enter into his kingdom. And the sun rises in the east! " The Russian revolution," wrote Lenin in August, 1917, "must be regarded as a link in the chain of socialist proletarian revolutions which will result from the imperialist war." That is the historical significance of the Great War. It has hastened the collapse of capitalism; it has speeded up the industrial developments which are to be at once the main causes of that collapse and the main factors in socialist reconstruction; and it has made plain to all who can read the signs of the times that socialism could only come about through a series of world-wide revolutionary explosions.

Right-wing socialism, the socialism of social solidarity and the enlightened human reason, the socialism that was to be secured by permeation and to be maintained by the favour of a caste of Fabian experts, was the natural outgrowth of the era when textile capital was

SIGNIFICANCE OF THE GREAT WAR 89

dominant. But we have entered upon a sterner age, the age of iron and steel. " Modern imperialism," writes Boudin, the American Marxist, " is the politico-social expression of the economic fact that iron and steel have taken the place of textiles as the leading industry of capitalism. And imperialism means war. Textiles, therefore, mean peace ; iron and steel—war." There is a large measure of truth in Boudin's views ; and from this outlook we see, as Walton Newbold has been proclaiming all through the war, that one of the main causes of the contest has been the need for the raw materials wherewith capitalist imperialism retains its power, the need of the rival groups for iron and steel, for coal, for mineral oil, and so on. Exploitation has taken on new forms ; capitalism draws its strength from new sources ; therewith the capitalist world has passed away from the peaceful ideals of the Manchester school, has turned back to high protection, offensive and defensive alliances, and the devotion of all the resources of science to securing preparedness for war. Then comes the explosion ; if it had not come over Serbia and Belgium, it would presumably have come over something equally remote from the underlying real cause of the war. But these might-have-beens need not detain us. The war came as the climax of the era of capitalist imperialism ; it put a final term to Manchesterism and to the types of socialism that were in truth no more than outgrowths of mid-Victorian Cobdenism. Fabianism was the socialist counterpart

CREATIVE REVOLUTION

to the doctrine of peaceful penetration. Zimmerwaldianism, bolshevism, class-war socialism pushed to its logical extreme, is at once the outcome and the sole possible reply to militant and imperialist capitalism. The Cobdenites and the socialist inheritors of the Cobdenite tradition proclaimed that this was the War Which Would End War. Few imperialists believed the shibboleth which not a few among them found it convenient to reiterate ; those who did believe it, whether in the Allied or in the Central camp, were looking to an armed peace secured and upheld by the might of a victorious group of exploiters. But to revolutionary socialists it seems that the only war that will end war is the class war, fought out to its ultimate issue ; and those alone who are robust of mind, keen of vision, and bold and constructive of imagination, can hearken gladly to the sounds of joyance, can preserve their confident assurance "that the rages of the ages shall be cancelled, and deliverance offered from the darts that were." For these know that, come what may, it is likely that the world has yet to pass through a terrible time, to endure perchance a worse ordeal than that of the past five years. That is why we point to the parallels of the barbarian invasions, the wars of religion, and the Napoleonic campaigns. We do not expect the great change from capitalism to communism, from democracy to ergatocracy, to be carried through without a world convulsion ; we have but a faint hope that the worst stages have already been

SIGNIFICANCE OF THE GREAT WAR 91

overpassed. But the outstanding difference between this change and the earlier ones lies in the new factor of communist intelligence. The revolutionary impulse, the will to change, urges mankind along the forward road made ready by the processes of economic evolution, by the development of the material conditions of production ; but progress is no longer blind, for to-day we see consciousness the will informing, helping mightily in the work of creative revolution.

It is interesting to find that in the first year of the war, and long before the 1917 revolution, Leon Trotsky, then an obscure exile, gave expression to the substance of the ideas we have been endeavouring to convey in this chapter, and emphasised the greatness of the creative task awaiting the constructive energies of revolutionary socialists. At the close of the pamphlet *War or Revolution* he showed that the struggle between competing imperialisms, whatever its immediate issue, would bring the capitalist world face to face with the alternative of permanent war or revolution. " The revolutionary epoch will create new forms of organisation out of the inexhaustible resources of working-class socialism ; new forms that will be equal to the greatness of the new tasks. To this work we will apply ourselves at once, amid the rattling of the machine guns, the crashing of cathedrals, and the howling of the jackals of capitalism. Amid this hellish orchestra of death, we will keep our minds clear, our

92 CREATIVE REVOLUTION

vision undimmed. We feel that we ourselves are the only creative force of the future. Already there are more of us than it may seem. To-morrow there will be more of us than to-day. And the day after to-morrow, millions will rise up under our banner, millions who even now, sixty-seven years after the publication of the Communist Manifesto, have nothing to lose but their chains."

Yet more striking were the words of Rosa Luxemburg, spoken in what we believe to have been her last important public utterance. She was murdered on January 15, 1919. At the inaugural meeting of the Communist Party of Germany (Spartacus Group), held in Berlin during the last three days of December, 1918, she made an impassioned speech in support of the Spartacist programme, a speech shortly to appear in English as a pamphlet, entitled *Revolutionary Socialism in Action.* A few extracts may be strung together: " To-day we can seriously set about destroying capitalism once for all. Nay more, not merely is this our duty to the proletariat, but our solution offers the only means of saving human society from destruction. . . . Socialism is inevitable, not merely because proletarians are no longer willing to live under the conditions imposed by the capitalist class ; but further, because, if the proletariat fails to fulfil its duty as a class, if it fails to realise socialism, we shall crash down together to a common doom." But the transition is not to be effected without suffering.

SIGNIFICANCE OF THE GREAT WAR 98

" Socialism will not be and cannot be inaugurated by decrees. . . . Socialism must be created by the masses, must be made by every proletarian. Where the chains of capitalism are forged, there must the chains be broken. . . . Thus only can socialism be brought into being. . . . The conclusion to be drawn is, not only that during the second act of tne revolution strikes will become increasingly prevalent ; but further, that strikes will become the central feature and the decisive factors of the revolution, thrusting purely political questions into the background. The inevitable consequence of this will be that the struggle in the economic field will be enormously intensified." Finally, speaking of training for the struggle, she comes to the Bergsonian position that life is action : " The masses must learn how to use power, by using power." It is not a question of educating the proletariat by theory, of delivering speeches, of disseminating leaflets and pamphlets. " The workers, to-day, will learn in the school of action."

CHAPTER SIX

**THE
RUSSIAN
REVOLUTION**

Russia will never be for half-measures. Russia will not make a revolution simply in order to get rid of Tsar Nicholas and to replace him by tsar-deputies, tsar-judges, and tsar-policemen.

ALEXANDER HERZEN (1851).

It is pleasanter and more useful to live through the experience of a revolution than to write about one.

NICOLAI LENIN (Dec. 12, 1917)

CHAPTER SIX

THE RUSSIAN REVOLUTION

PERHAPS the first and last lesson of the Russian revolution is " Thorough," if we may borrow the watchword of a great reactionary. But in more detailed consideration, writing on the second anniversary of the bolshevik revolution, we may speak of three chief lessons taught by that volcanic upheaval and its consequences: (1) the futility of Tolstoyan pacifism; (2) the supreme value of the soviet as a revolutionary instrument; and (3) the need for a Third International to replace the dead and rotting Second International and as a countercheck quarrelsome to the capitalist League of Nations. There have of course been many other stirring phenomena bearing a Russian imprint, but most of these are no more than local features of the world-wide revolutionary movement, and are not specifically Russian. Even the soviet is not exclusively Russian in origin. Moreover, the function of the soviet as revolutionary instrument and as the basis of a new political synthesis will come up for discussion in a later chapter. But Russia has been (after Gallilee and England) the chief home of the gospel of non-resistance. To-day when we think of pacifism, we think first of Tolstoy, rather than of

7

98   CREATIVE REVOLUTION

the Society of Friends, or of Christ the Essene who bade us turn the other cheek to the smiter. Yet it is from Russia, within a few years of Tolstoy's death, that has come the splendid vital impetus of fighting revolutionism; and from Moscow was issued in March, 1919, *The New Communist Manifesto*. The Third International will be dealt with in the next chapter. Here we are chiefly concerned with the bearing of the Russian revolution on the problem of pacifism. But first, some historic parallels may help to a clearer understanding of the significance of the Russian revolution.

The English " revolution," which opened the series of the great bourgeois revolutions in Europe, was a protracted process, and may be said to have taken four centuries to consummate. Those whose interest is focussed on striking but in truth superficial political changes, think of the civil war in the middle of the seventeenth century, or of the final expulsion of the Stuarts and the establishment of " constitutional parliamentary government " in the close of the same century, as predominant revolutionary phases, so that the events of 1688 are commonly spoken of as preeminently the English revolution. But the socialist historian of the future will regard the whole epoch from the end of the Wars of the Roses with the founding of the Tudor monarchy in 1509, down to the inauguration in Britain of something really resembling universal suffrage by the Representation of the People Act of 1918—he will regard the whole

THE RUSSIAN REVOLUTION 99

of this historic phase, with its interassociated economic and political changes, as comprising the British bourgeois revolution. Similarly with France. There the process was comparatively rapid, yet it occupied nearly a century. The " French revolution " was not completed by a single episode. Striking as were the political changes effected, for instance, on the momentous night of August 4, 1789, this was not the French revolution ; nor was the revolution completed by the rise of Napoleon to power ; nor even by the events of 1830 and of 1848. The French revolution lasted from the summoning of the States General in 1789 down to the final consolidation of the power of the third bourgeois republic in 1875. The French revolution was the work of an entire century.

We can, in imagination, and with the aid of the socialist criticism of which Marx was the supreme exponent, look upon such great changes with the eye of the dispassionate historian of a future age. But these are the times that try men's souls. It is far harder to contemplate in a similar historical perspective the events of the Russian revolution, the prelude to a universal communist revolution. Yet as we look back upon the brief period since the inauguration of soviet rule on November 7, 1917, it becomes obvious that the Russian revolution deserves the name of revolution in a much fuller sense than does either of the great secular movements known respectively as the French revolution and the English revolution.

100 CREATIVE REVOLUTION

And this not merely because the Russian revolution is the only sort of revolution which interests us as communists, because it is a revolution which aims at and bids fair to succeed in the final abolition of ownership rule throughout a large and populous area ; but because it is a sudden and extensive change, simultaneously affecting the whole substance of society as well as the political forms. If all goes well, our hypothetical future historian will be able to look upon the Russian revolution of 1917 as the inception of the world-wide social revolution, to be completed, we hope and believe, within our own lifetime, and perhaps in the very near future. But for us, who actually live in the rapids of revolution, one phase in particular stands out when we envisage the Russian revolution. We think of the establishment of the soviet power on November 7, 1917, and we think of the titanic struggle to uphold and consolidate that power during the two years that have elapsed since then. We British bolsheviks think above all of the bolshevik revolution. We recognise that the main drive of the whole revolutionary movement of 1917 came from the war-weariness of the Russian army and the Russian people. We realise that the teachings of Tolstoy, in conjunction with the experience of intolerable hardships and the reaction against unnamable horrors, were the chief immediate causes of the fall of the tsarist regime. Yet we know that neither the first revolution of 1917, nor the second, was pacifist. The

THE RUSSIAN REVOLUTION 101

bourgeois imperialists of the first stage wished to go on fighting for the aims of the secret treaties, and this, as much as anything, led to the second, the real revolution. But the sovietists have proved doughty fighters. They have been forced by circumstances into an attitude which has nothing in common with the principle of non-resistance.

Perhaps during the opening phases of the war few of us in the left wing were entirely free from the illusions of pacifism. The hatred that every civilised human being feels for war, the clear recognition that the war was the outcome of decades of capitalist rivalries and that it was a mere accident which of the Powers had thrown the spark into the powder-barrel, these and many other considerations inspired a revolt against war in general. We cared little whether the Austrian quarrel with Serbia, the alleged German scheme for world-domination, Russian designs on Constantinople and the panicky Russian mobilisation ; any one of half a dozen squabbles over raw materials in Lorraine, in Mesopotamia, or in Persia ; British navalism versus German militarism—we cared little whether this or any other of the alleged causes was the " real cause " of the war. We laughed with the same bitterness at the British indictment of Germany and at the German indictment of Britain ; we were equally bored by all the propagandist literature with which the capitalist governments endeavoured to stimulate the war passions of their respective subjects ; we drowsed

102 CREATIVE REVOLUTION

indifferently over the official publications, white or black, violet, indigo, or blue, green, yellow, orange, or red. Chromatic war literature left us cold. We felt with Karl Liebknecht : " The present war is not a war for the defence of national integrity, nor for the liberation of down-trodden peoples, nor for the benefit of the masses. From the point of view of the proletariat, it only signifies the greatest possible concentration and intensification of political oppression, of economic exploitation, and of the wholesale military slaughter of the working classes for the benefit of capitalism and absolutism." We felt with Karl Liebknecht that our business as socialists was in each country to attack the enemy, imperialism. The British socialists should not, at long range, fire volleys of abuse at German imperialism ; they should train their guns upon the capitalist imperialism with which they were best acquainted by personal experience. British socialists should, above all in wartime, talk of British tyranny and British misrule. And conversely. Liebknecht faithfully followed his own rede, and paid in years of imprisonment, followed by a brief but glorious interlude of liberty when, as he imagined, the day of the people had dawned for Germany. He fell in the end beneath the bludgeoning of the militarist butchers, and alleged socialists looked on the while well-contented at the removal of the dangerous Spartacist agitator. But to return to the Great War, we of the left wing were war-weary before the war had even begun !

THE RUSSIAN REVOLUTION   103

Yet the essence of our antagonism was not pacifist. In this country the pacifists to-day are not found among the communists of the left wing. Our point was that the war was not our war. We would have nothing to do with the " political truce." It might be in-expedient, in a war-mad world, in a world suffering from a virulent epidemic of nationalist fever, to court imprisonment or lynching by public demonstrations of internationalism or anti-patriotism. At any rate we would take no part in nationalist struggles. We would bide our time, until the nationalist fever had abated, and until the economic changes resulting from the war had made the workers ready to hearken to internationalist and communist propaganda. We in England were refused passports to attend the congresses of Zimmerwald and Kiental where the class-war attitude was affirmed by left-wing socialists of all other lands, predominently in-fluenced by Russian refugees. But the censor-ship was less strict than it became in the later years of the war, and we were able through the post to send in our individual adhesion to Zimmerwald and to receive for a time the issues of the Zimmerwald " Bulletin " ; sometimes in French or German, and sometimes in the quaint but forceful English with which the polyglot Russian revolutionists have, since November, 1917, made all the world familiar. Others besides the class-war socialists sent in their adhesion to Zimmerwald. One of the greatest jokes in history is that the I.L.P., fundamentally

104   CREATIVE REVOLUTION

pacifist, likewise supported Zimmerwald and Kiental, falsely imagining that the anti-war demonstrations of Zimmerwald and Kiental had a Tolstoyan foundation! This conception of the I.L.P. outlook towards Zimmerwald, formed by the writers at the time, is interestingly confirmed by Grumbach, an independent observer, resident in Switzerland throughout the war, and equally hostile to pacifism and to what he terms "the error of Zimmerwald–Kiental." Writing of the I.L.P. and of the B.S.P. [erroneously in the latter case] he says: "What then was the upshot of the adhesion of these parties to Zimmerwald? It was a pacifist demonstration, and in the Kiental ledger it must be entered on the debit side of the account." Among the actual participants in the strangely mingled conferences of Zimmerwald and Kiental there were doubtless not a few genuine pacifists. But the leading thought of the conferences was that socialists had no concern with this war, since it was a capitalist quarrel; and that the socialists who championed the right of "national defence" in such a capitalist quarrel were deserting the red flag in favour of the nationalist banner. Yet Trotsky and Lenin, the life and soul of Zimmerwald and Kiental, are anything but pacifists. Trotsky, who may be described as being, next to Liebknecht, the most pronounced anti-militarist in Europe, has become bolshevik commissary for war, and has organised the Red Army thanks to which the soviet power has been able to maintain itself throughout

THE RUSSIAN REVOLUTION 105

two stormful years. Trotsky would not fight on behalf of Russian imperialism ; but he will fight to the death on behalf of the Russian Socialist Federative Soviet Republic. Trotsky has coined a striking phrase in refutation of the teaching of the Tolstoyans. "They tell us to disarm," he said in April, 1918. "When attacked by wolves, they would turn to lay their own wolves' teeth upon the shelf ! " Nor is Lenin less remote from pacifism. Look, for example, at the pamphlet on *Socialism and the War* issued by Lenin and Zinoviev in the year 1915. In the section on " Offensive and Defensive Wars " we read : " If to-morrow Morocco were to enter the war against France, India against England, Persia and China against Russia, these subordinate struggles would be legitimate wars of defence, regardless of the question who had begun the fighting." Grumbach, in the pamphlet already referred to, finds it easy to make fun of Lenin. "Madness," writes the Alsatian socialist, " is here exalted into a method. Colonies may legitimately wage offensive wars. Lenin would like to swing himself across a barbary steed, to wrap himself in a white burnoose, and to sally forth with the Moroccans against the French, muttering veritable bolshevist spells the while, and desiring to defend the independence of his majesty the sultan of Marrakesh and Fez, and the independence of his majesty's subjects. But when the greatest republic in Europe (a land which, despite the capitalist defects from which it

106   CREATIVE REVOLUTION

suffers in common with all the countries of the capitalist world, deserves to be described politically as a democracy), when this democratic republic takes up arms against the invading legions of the feudalist German monarchy, . . . and when French socialists lend their aid to the defence of their country, then Lenin, with immaculate bolshevist zeal, empties the vials of his wrath upon the devoted heads of the misguided ' socialist patriots.' "

Well, well ! These were difficult questions throughout the early years of the war, and few of us can claim to have been consistent all the time, unless it be the unmitigated Germanophobes on the one side, the unmitigated Anglophobes, Gallophobes, and Russophobes on the other side, and the unqualified Tolstoyans in both camps. Yet many of us in these isles shared Lenin's generous illusions, if illusions they be, regarding the subject nationalities. Even avowed pacifists, in April, 1916, wished success to the Irish rebellion, in which so outspoken a pacifist as Sheehy-Skeffington met his death no less than such ardent fighters as Jim Connolly and Padraic Pearse ; and many of us who regard all nationalism as medieval were almost ready, for the time being, to exchange the red flag for the green. Did we not remember the words written in 1869 by Marx, that the British workers will never achieve, and will never deserve to achieve, their own independence until they have the spirit to fight for the independence of their Irish brethren ? Half a century ago Karl Marx was a Sinn Feiner !

THE RUSSIAN REVOLUTION 107

As to consistency, if we believed with Lenin that the war marked the final phase of capitalism, and that the fratricidal struggle would entail the final collapse of bourgeois dominion, should we not, recognising at an early date with Hamon that the outcome of the war must inevitably be universal revolution, and that the longer the war lasted the greater would be the speeding-up process in the march towards revolution—should we not have been willing, nay eager, to take part in the war ? Yet many of us could not accept that horn of the dilemma. Anything but pacifist, we said : " No capitalist government shall constrain us to take up arms in a capitalist quarrel. Let the capitalists and their bondsmen fight matters out. We are freemen, and we will reserve our energies for the only war that matters." When the time is ripe, the master class will have plenty of reason to understand that we are not pacifists, that our spirit is not that of those who turn the other cheek to the smiter. It is learning the lesson apace ; and it will learn, as soon as the class consciousness of the workers is thoroughly awakened, that every attempt at repression will serve merely to fan the fires of intelligent revolt.

But the great object lesson of the Russian revolution has made it much easier for us to take a clear and consistent view of this international communist line of conduct, which is equally remote from the blind war-fever of the misguided " patriot," ignorant tool in the hands of his capitalist master, and from the

108 CREATIVE REVOLUTION

non-resistance of the Tolstoyan pacifist. We know that were we now in Russia we should be fighting for the defence of the Soviet Republic, whereas, were the Great War to recur (as it would to-morrow owing to intensified capitalist rivalries were it not for the utter exhaustion of the combatants), not one of us who take the international communist view would raise a finger in the defence of any capitalist state, whether it call itself feudalist or democratic, and whether it be republic or monarchy. The Russian revolution has simplified the issues, so that he who runs may read. For us there is only one war, that of labour against capital. We pursue our aims wherever possible by the peaceful methods of workers organising in new and more effective ways. Direct action need not necessarily lead to bloodshed. But fight we shall, if fight we must, to promote the coming of ergatocracy. If the possessing classes revive their scheme of organising black hundreds and giving them the question-begging name of " citizen guards," or if, after a bloodless revolution here (as after the practically bloodless revolution in Petrograd in November, 1917), the forces of capitalist reaction at home and abroad combine in an endeavour to destroy us, we shall apply the lesson of the Russian revolution and shall consolidate our defences by the inauguration of Red Guards and the creation of a Red Army. The day for pacifism will not come until *all* the hnads of the capitalist hydra have been cut off. Such is the teaching of the years 1917 to 1920.

CHAPTER SEVEN

**THE
THIRD
INTERNATIONAL**

The Second International is not merely dead but damned. . . . The success of the working-class movement . . . is inseparably connected with the success of the new Red or Moscow International. . . . The only practicable " socialist unity " is the unified activity of the revolutionary left wing.

SHOW YOUR COLOURS
(a personal manifesto issued in May, 1919).

CHAPTER SEVEN

THE THIRD INTERNATIONAL

ONE of the main contentions of this little volume has been that social solidarity is impossible under capitalism, and cannot be achieved until after the social revolution has entirely abolished class. And since the cleavage in the socialist ranks takes place along the plane of separation between those who believe that a working social solidarity already exists, and those who contend that the class struggle runs athwart the whole structure of contemporary society, it follows that socialist unity in the full sense of the term is a chimera. The Second International was an International of socialist parliamentarians, who thought that parliament was, or might become, an effective expression of the hypothetical communal will. The Third International is an International of revolutionary socialists who consider parliament effete ; who believe that class-conscious workers must deliberately override what is spoken of as the popular will, in so far as that will is the expression of capitalist ideology, and of capitalist-imposed illusions concerning the structure of bourgeois society ; whose analysis of contemporary tendencies convinces them that soviets

112　　CREATIVE REVOLUTION

must be the main instruments of revolution and the basis of communist reconstruction; who are no longer social democrats but communist ergatocrats; who feel assured that we must pass through dictatorship to ergatocracy. Where a united socialist party already exists, as in Italy and France, a semblance of unity may be retained for a time while the party as a whole moves to the left, while the Second International is repudiated in favour of the Third, and while even the parliamentary deputies renounce the institution through which they are supposed to be working. But in Great Britain, where socialist unity has never existed even in name, no one out of Bedlam can suppose it possible, at this juncture, to unite under one banner all the discrepant activities of those who here profess and call themselves socialists. The Labour Party will continue its adhesion to the corpse of the Second International, and the socialist apostles of social solidarity and parliamentary democracy will continue their adhesion to the Labour Party. But communist ergatocrats will unite on the platform of the Third International.

It is needless, in such a study as the present, to attempt a history of the foundation of the Moscow International. An account by an eyewitness, an Englishman who was on the spot in Moscow during the first week of March, 1919, will be found in the closing pages of Ransome's *Six Weeks in Russia*. The only British socialist, so far as we know, to participate actively was

THE THIRD INTERNATIONAL 118

Fineberg, a member of the B.S.P., and perhaps ere long we shall have from him an inside story of the proceedings. As regards the actual basis of the new International, one of the most useful publications as yet available in English is W. Paul's *The New Communist Manifesto*.

In its preamble, the new manifesto refers to the *Manifesto of the Communist Party* drawn up seventy-two years earlier by Marx and Engels. The new manifestants are the successors of the old. "Our duty," they say, "is to gather together the revolutionary experience of the working classes, to purge the movement from opportunism and nationalist influences, to unite the forces of all genuinely revolutionary parties in the world proletariat, and thereby to facilitate and hasten the victory of the communist revolution." The general principles that will guide the communists in their advance towards the goal are summarised under six heads :

(1) The crisis into which the world has been brought by the war can be solved in one way only, by THE DICTATORSHIP OF THE PROLETARIAT. The class-conscious workers "will introduce a general obligation to work and a regime of discipline in work. Thus within a few short years, they will not only heal the gaping wounds caused by the war, but will raise mankind to heights hitherto undreamed of."

(2) Substantially, this section declares that the only possible league of nations is A WORLD-WIDE FEDERATION OF SOVIET REPUBLICS.

(3) This section demands GENUINE SELF-

8

114 CREATIVE REVOLUTION

GOVERNMENT FOR ALL COLONIES. "Whereas capitalist Europe forces the most backward parts of the world into the maelstrom of capitalism, socialist Europe will be a true helper to the newly liberated colonies. The superior technical knowledge, the improved organising capacity, and the spiritual influences radiating from a socialised Europe, will facilitate the methodical adoption of socialist institutions. Slaves of the colonies in Africa and Asia, the hour of proletarian dictatorship in Europe will be the hour of your release!"

(4) THE RULE OF THE PROLETARIAT CANNOT BE ESTABLISHED THROUGH THE METHODS OF BOURGEOIS DEMOCRACY. "It creates conditions and forms for the realisation of a new and higher type of political institutions—proletarian democracy." [Read "ergatocracy!"] . . . "In this realm of destruction, where not only the means of production and transport, but also the institutions of political democracy, lie shattered and bleeding, THE PROLETARIAT MUST CREATE ITS OWN APPARATUS, which, above all, must serve as a means of reunion for the working classes, and must enable them to effect a revolutionary intervention on behalf of the further development of mankind. THE WORKERS' COUNCILS, THE SOVIETS, CONSTITUTE THIS APPARATUS, . . . WHICH IS THE MOST POWERFUL WEAPON IN THE HANDS OF THE PROLETARIAT TO-DAY."

(5) "The outcry of the bourgeois world against civil war and the Red Terror is the most outrageous hyprocrisy ever known in the history

THE THIRD INTERNATIONAL   115

of political struggles. There would be no civil war if the profiteering cliques which have brought mankind to the verge of ruin did not do their utmost to oppose the progress of the working masses, if they did not engineer conspiracy and subsidise murder, if they did not seek armed assistance from other lands in order to maintain or restore their predatory privileges. CIVIL WAR IS FORCED UPON THE WORKING CLASSES BY THEIR MORTAL ENEMIES. Unless they would prove faithless to themselves and their future, which is also the future of all mankind, THE WORKERS MUST RETURN BLOW FOR BLOW. . . . Hence it is necessary to disarm the bourgeoisie and to arm the proletariat. . . . THE SOVIET ARMY IS INDISPENSABLE TO THE SOVIET STATE."

(6) The socialist centre, which is endeavouring to restore the Second International, must be repudiated no less than those sections of the socialist right which, throughout the war, supported their respective governments of capitalist and imperialist warmongers. The First International foresaw coming developments and began to drive a wedge. The Second International helped to organise millions of proletarians. THE THIRD INTERNATIONAL ADVOCATES THE DIRECT ACTION OF THE REVOLUTIONARY PROLETARIAT. "Proletarians of all lands, unite against imperialist barbarism, against monarchy, against the privileged classes, against the bourgeois state and bourgeois property, against every kind and every manifestation of social and national oppression. Proletarians of all lands,

116 CREATIVE REVOLUTION

flock to the banner of the soviets, and fight the revolutionary fight for the power of the workers and the dictatorship of the proletariat."

It is sufficiently clear from the foregoing abstract of *The New Communist Manifesto*, that the document emphasises what we have already explained to be the three crowning achievements of the Russian revolution : the dispelling of the illusion of pacifism ; the adoption of the soviet as the supreme instrument of revolutionary transformation ; and the creation of the Third International. The touchstone for the adherents of the Third International is the acceptance, not only of the tactic of the class struggle, but also of the policy of the dictatorship of the proleteriat. The aim of the Third International, the aim of those left-wing socialist and communist organisations that have endorsed its policy and sent in their formal adhesion, is something utterly different from democracy in any sense in which that term has hitherto been understood. Their aim is not " social democracy " at all. Democracy is a back number. Their aim is the type of social organisation to which in this study we have given the name of communist ergatocracy.

From the nature of the circumstances, it was impossible that the gathering of revolutionists who founded the Third International could be " representative " in any formal sense of the term. In Moscow, the bolshevik capital, the Russian soviet power, which had been the moving spirit in the whole affair, was sufficiently

THE THIRD INTERNATIONAL 117

represented by those who, increasingly supported
by all shades of socialist opinion in Russia, had
imposed the dictatorship of the proletariat in
November, 1917. Albrecht was there for the
German Spartacists ; Platten from Switzerland ;
Stang from Norway ; and Grinlund from Sweden ;
on behalf of the extreme left in their respective
lands. Those in the polyglot group who spoke
for other countries, for Ukraine, for the United
States, and so on, had of course no mandate.
Nor had Sadoul, a bold deserter from the French
military mission, though subsequent events have
endowed his position in Russia with quasi-
representative importance. Quite recently Fritz
Adler, belated apostle of an impracticable
" socialist unity," but a man incapable of deliberate misstatement, could write in " Der Kampf " :
" As the Lucerne congress proved, the majority
of the world proletariat shares the point of view
of the real [!] socialists. . . . The Third International, in spite of its undeniable revolutionary
strength, is nevertheless weak. With the ex-
ception of Italy, the Third International has
practically no adherents in Western Europe.
Moreover, the Italians are, on the whole, in
actual practice, much nearer to Longuet's
position than to that of Lenin. . . . In fact it
is a question of tactics rather than a question
of principles that has led to the secession of
many parties from the Second International."
It is hardly necessary, at this stage of our argument, to reiterate the conviction animating the
present writers that the differences to-day

118 CREATIVE REVOLUTION

between the left wing and the right in the socialist movement are no mere differences of tactics, but are profound differences of sociological principle. When Adler speaks of the views held by " the majority of the world proletariat," we would ask him whether he refers to those who are proletarian by status merely, or to those who are proletarian by revolutionary conviction? The distinction is vital. The essence of the left-wing philosophy is that upon the latter alone, upon the proletarians by revolutionary conviction, depends the possibility of the social revolution. The socialism represented at Lucerne was what Marx long ago named " petty bourgeois socialism." This is the socialism that is now, in England, achieving striking Labour victories in parliamentary by-elections, the socialism that has secured sweeping majorities in many of the borough councils. But it is not the socialism of the revolutionary proletariat, which in spirit, if not in material fact, was represented in the formation of the Red or Moscow International.

As we write, it is less than a year since the Third International was founded. In view of the difficulties of communication in a distracted, war-worn, and famine-stricken Europe, there has hardly been time for the issues to clear. But it is not true that, apart from Italy, the Third International has practically no adherents in Western Europe. The British are proverbially slow to move, and here we have no socialist unity, whether of the right wing

THE THIRD INTERNATIONAL 119

or of the left. But *The New Communist Manifesto* has hastened the cleavage between the right wing and the left, and has greatly improved the prospects of a left-wing consolidation. We may hope that ere long the new Communist International will be reinforced by the adhesion of a strong British section. The Independent Socialist Party of Germany has now decided to affiliate. In Holland, in Norway, and in Sweden, the respective socialist parties have joined the Third International, and the continued movement to the left tends increasingly to make the affiliation effective. Further support comes from Greece, Spain, Chili, China, and the American I.W.W. The French Socialist Party is, like the British Labour Party, essentially a parliamentary group whose policy is guided with an eye to success at the polls. But even in France, alike in socialist and in syndicalist circles, the spirit of the Third International is widely diffused—and France, it must be remembered, occupies the place of honour in respect of mutinies in favour of the " Hands off Russia " movement.

But let us turn to Adler's test case, that of Italy. The Italians, he tells us, are in practice far more inclined to sympathise with the views of " real socialists " like Jean Longuet and Ramsay MacDonald, than with socialists of the Lenin type, who have " forgotten Marx's teaching." At the Italian Socialist Congress, held in Bologna during the beginning of October, 1919, even the right-wing resolution, which

120 CREATIVE REVOLUTION

secured a third of the votes, called for "the adoption of the soviet principle." Bordiga, of the left wing, moved a resolution demanding that the party should in future be known as the Communist Party of Italy, demanding abstention from the elections and from parliament, and the expulsion from the party of all those who believe in bourgeois democracy and all those who repudiate the necessity for an armed fight against the bourgeoisie in order to establish the dictatorship of the proletariat. This drastic proposal secured little more than one-twentieth of the votes. The centre motion, that of Serrati, which was carried by an overwhelming majority, while not desiring so extreme a measure as the expulsion of dissentients, proclaimed that the Russian revolution had been "the most fortunate event in the history of the workers"; advocated communist ideas substantially identical with those expounded in this book; announced the adhesion of the party to the Third International; and, while deciding to participate in elections for propaganda purposes, declared its policy in the following terms:

"The conference recognises that the present organs of local and national government cannot be transformed into instruments for liberating the workers; that such organs must be replaced by workers', soldiers', and peasants' councils, workers' economic councils, and so on. The councils, functioning at first under capitalist domination, will be instruments in the forcible

THE THIRD INTERNATIONAL 121

war of liberation, and will subsequently become the organs of social and economic transformation, the organs for reconstruction in the communist social order. The forcible conquest of power by the workers will establish the temporary dictatorship of the proletariat."

Events are moving fast in Italy, and a moderate view is that the " abstentionists " from parliamentary and municipal activity will dominate next year's congress. But Bordiga believes that the revolution will have occurred in Italy before next year's socialist congress can take place.— So much for Adler's fantastic misconception as to the dynamic of the Italian movement.

It will be noted that the only serious tactical difference between the centre and the left wing of the Italian Socialist Party, sections which taken in conjunction correspond to the extreme left in our own land, concerns the question of the " abstentionist " policy of the Bordiga group. Throughout the Third International this is the only important matter upon which no unanimity has been secured. Our personal view, for instance, is that, whilst " abstentionism " undoubtedly has a somewhat impossibilist flavour in tranquil times, when the likelihood of a sudden collapse of the old order seems remote, most of those who believe the hour of revolutionary change to be at hand will regard participation in parliamentary and municipal activities as sheer waste of time and energy, and as tending to promote confusionism. But no party could wisely attempt to dictate to

122 CREATIVE REVOLUTION

individual members as to whether they should or should not accept the abstentionist view; no party could profitably impose a test which it would be impossible to enforce. The tactical question concerns only the participation of the party, *as a party*, in electoral strife. Many even of those who believe that the decisive hour is upon us, are of opinion that abstentionism implies renunciation of valuable opportunities for propaganda. Such, we gather, is the opinion of Lenin. Here there is no radical divergence of principle, such as exists between the revolutionary communists who expect a sudden transformation establishing the dictatorship of the proletariat on the way to ergatocracy, and the socialists who hope to achieve socialism by a tranquil, painless, and evolutionary change, through the intermediation of the existing political institutions of capitalist society. The question of abstentionism versus participation for propaganda purposes will not be made a test question either in the Third International or in any of its branches; and differences of opinion on this head will not interfere with the unification of left-wing forces in Great Britain. A conceivable compromise is the adoption of " Sinn Fein tactics " by the communist left wing. Candidates will then be run for propaganda purposes, but will not, if elected, take their seats at Westminster. Is it not even possible that in Britain, no less than as Bordiga anticipates in Italy, the speeding-up of the historical process, the fatal embarrassments of

THE THIRD INTERNATIONAL 123

capitalism, and the strengthening of the revolutionary will of the masses, may render the problem obsolete before it has been seriously faced ? More probably, however, Great Britain has to experience the phase of labourism or bastard socialism. In Russia the revolution was made in two stages, and it was not until after eight months of half-measures that the regime of the Laodiceans fell before the onslaughts of the uncompromising bolsheviks. Ebert's administration, sitting on bayonets, may be overthrown at any moment by a Spartacist revolt more fortunate and more opportune than that of January, 1919—though in Germany an interlude of monarchical restoration seems more probable. Here in Britain there is considerable reason to suppose that the revolution will take place against a Labour government which will have failed hopelessly, with its Fabian policy and its semi-bourgeois outlook, to cope with the disastrous heritage of capitalist imperialism. In vague outline only can we foresee the future, but we can at least endeavour to make ready for imminent possibilities.

In closing this chapter, a few words may be permitted as a tribute to some of those of whom we cannot fail to think as we call to mind the socialist history of the last two years. We have no particular fondness for meditations among the tombs. We do not love to dwell on memories of the dead. It is our joy, rather, to talk, living, to the living ; to say with William

124 CREATIVE REVOLUTION

Kingdon Clifford "Let us take hands and help, for this day we are alive together." That is how, it is our delight to believe, the young and vigorous, to whom the world belongs, will march lustily forward when our own last sun has set ! And yet we cannot but think, in this momentous hour, when the Soviet Republic is still facing a world in arms, of those comrades who have so recently fallen or been struck down by the way. We think of Karl Liebknecht and Rosa Luxemburg ; of Leon Tychko (Yogehes) and Tybor Samuelli ; of the prisoners butchered by Kolchak and Denikin ; of the countless Russian, Finnish, and Hungarian victims of the White Terror. All these are the " foreign " comrades of those who in truth know nothing of national distinctions. Here in England the day has not yet dawned for anything more serious than a few months in prison. But we of the British left wing, who do not seek a bloody revolution, yet do not fear it if bloody it must be ; we who know that no one is of value to the revolutionary movement who is not ready to go "over the top " when the tocsin sounds ; we know that when the time comes our own ranks will be thinned by the well-aimed fire of our misguided fellow-workers, the slaves of our capitalist foes. We know, too, that the dead will continue to work, as Jim Connolly works, as Rosa Luxemburg works, as many another dead comrade still works to-day for the cause of communism. We remember the words of Walt Whitman :

THE THIRD INTERNATIONAL 125

Those corpses of young men,
Those martyrs who hang from the gibbets, those hearts pierced
    by the grey lead,
Cold and motionless as they seem, live elsewhere with un-
    slaughtered vitality.
They live in other young men, O Kings !
They live in brothers ready to defy you,
They were purified by death, they were taught and exalted.
Not a grave of the murdered for freedom but grows seed for
    freedom, in its turn to bear seed,
Which the winds carry afar and resow, and the rains and the
    snows nourish.
Not a disembodied spirit can the weapons of tyrants let loose
But it stalks invisibly over the earth, whispering, counselling,
    cautioning.

CHAPTER EIGHT

THE
DICTATORSHIP
OF THE
PROLETARIAT

The dictatorship of the proletariat is the organisation of the advance-guard of the oppressed as the ruling class, for the purpose of crushing the oppressors.

NICOLAI LENIN.

CHAPTER EIGHT

THE DICTATORSHIP OF THE PROLETARIAT

THE question of the dictatorship of the proletariat is one of the main issues dividing the revolutionary and socialist left wing from the evolutionary and parliamentarian right. Indeed, to many it seems the most important of all the tactical differences which separate the two schools of socialist thought. Officially, at least, the I.L.P. repudiates the dictatorship of the proletariat as it repudiates the tactic of the class struggle. On the other hand, all the left-wing socialist organisations in Britain, such as the Socialist Labour Party, the British Socialist Party, the Workers' Socialist Federation, and the South Wales Socialist Society, endorse the policy of the Third International. As we have seen, the first section of the New Communist Manifesto proclaims that the crisis into which the world has been brought by the war can be solved in one way only, by the dictatorship of the proletariat. It is the controversy of the hour between Kautsky and Lenin ; and the leading right-wing and the leading left-wing organisations in this country are appropriately engaged as we write in repub-

9

180 CREATIVE REVOLUTION

lishing in English the German's and the Russian's respective contributions to the discussion. Moreover, while it is a question of tactics, it is something more. In certain circumstances, quantitative differences tend with increase to become qualitative differences. A notable example is the matter of invested funds. A proletarian by status does not cease to be a proletarian merely because he has a hundred pounds or so in the savings bank or even in the war loan. It is a question of more or less; as soon as the point is reached when income from investment becomes the main source of livelihood, the quantitative difference has become qualitative, and the proletarian status has disappeared. In like manner, tactical differences, when sufficiently vital, become differences of principle, rendering united action difficult or impossible. Socialists must perforce take sides to-day over the question of the dictatorship of the proletariat; it is therefore absolutely essential that all socialists should understand clearly what this formidable phrase really means. Quite unauthoritatively, we will endeavour to define.

The word dictatorship is employed in the sense warranted by any dictionary. It signifies "absolute power, temporary or irregular, over a state, exercised by an individual, or by a group of individuals who form a minority." This definition rules out as sophistical the phrase often used in controversy by socialists who assert that the dictatorship of the proletariat is to replace "the dictatorship of the bour-

PROLETARIAN DICTATORSHIP 131

geoisie "; the latter term stretches unduly the signification of the word dictatorship. It is true that, under capitalism in its finished expression, the sway of the bourgeoisie is practically absolute — though the absoluteness is skilfully veiled by parliamentary forms. But bourgeois rule is now neither temporary nor irregular; it is a comparatively stable type of government throughout the final phases of capitalist evolution. It would be better to say that, during the revolutionary transition from parliamentary democracy to communist ergatocracy, the avowed dictatorship of the proletariat will replace the camouflaged oligarchy of the bourgeoisie.

What, in this connection, is meant by " proletariat " ? Consciously or unconsciously, all who conceive the dictatorship of the proletariat to be essential during transition, must use the word in a definitely restricted sense. Let us consider a crucial example. Despite the antithesis between " order " and " progress " to which reference was made in an earlier chapter, the revolutionary government will have to take stern measures to maintain order during the acute phases of the breakdown of capitalist society. Looting and acts of unorganised individual or mob violence will not be tolerated, and will be vigorously repressed by the Red Guard. Lenin, who is not simply a theoretical revolutionist, tells us that hooligans must be dealt with no less swiftly and mercilessly than exploiters. The hand of revolutionary authority will weigh heavily upon the counter-revolu-

132 CREATIVE REVOLUTION

tionary bourgeoisie, but it will weigh no less heavily upon the disorderly elements of proletarian society. The dictatorship of the proletariat does not mean a dictatorship exercised by the *Lumpenproletariat*. Nor does it mean a dictatorship exercised by those members of the proletariat (the majority under capitalism) whose mentality, whose ideology, remains more or less distinctively bourgeois. We do not advocate the dictatorship of proletarians who have not yet attained to class-consciousness, of the ragged-trousered philanthropists who in ordinary times accept with grumbling submissiveness the crumbs that fall from the master's table, saying "that's good enough for the likes of us." When hard days come, and when a revolutionary situation arises, these workers, who, as Stephen Reynolds phrases it "don' know 'xactly what they wants but wants it hellish bad for a long time," can perhaps achieve a revolt, but can never unguided, "undictatored," achieve a revolution. If we can conceive the absolute, temporary, and irregular rule of such elements as at all possible, we should not, by its establishment, have gone a step on the way to ergatocracy, but should merely have replaced democracy by ochlocracy—mob rule. Instead of passing through dictatorship to ergatocracy, we should pass through ochlocracy to chaos.

Revolutionists must know exactly what they want; they must not merely want it hellish bad for a long time. The absolute dominion during the period of transition must be exercised

PROLETARIAN DICTATORSHIP 133

by the organised, class-conscious elements within the ranks of those who, economically speaking, constitute the proletariat. Even within the domain of organised and class-conscious labour a further oligarchical restriction may be requisite, but of this anon. Sufficient for the moment to admit frankly that the absolute rule, temporary and irregular, will have to be a dictatorship *over* a large section of any proletariat. In the industrial field, the conception of the blackleg-proof union which underlies the guild socialist's transitional tactic, involves a similar unsparing control exercised by the more intelligent over the less intelligent elements of the proletariat. But it must never be forgotten that there are two fundamental differences between the bourgeois use of power and the proletarian. Proletarian dictatorship is avowedly temporary, whereas the bourgeois rulers regard their form of government as the final blossoming of human civilisation. Further, under bourgeois oligarchy, power is exercised by owners over non-owners, by exploiters over exploited ; under proletarian dictatorship, the rulers are the class-conscious workers, and their transitory rule is free from all taint of exploitation.

The need for dictatorship may be formulated from a somewhat different outlook, and this will throw further light upon the question of definition. Many socialists have felt that the difficulty of bringing about socialism may be thus stated : (1) a socialist commonwealth cannot be successfully inaugurated and carried on

134 CREATIVE REVOLUTION

except by socialists, by persons who have the socialist mentality; (2) but the socialist mentality cannot be acquired by the majority until the socialist commonwealth is already in being, for under capitalism average men and women have the mentality engendered by capitalist conditions. This looks like a deadlock, and it would in fact be a deadlock did not the dictatorship of the class-conscious proletariat offer an issue. A revolutionary situation will arise when the capitalist system is breaking down from the cumulative effect of its own inherent weaknesses. Concomitantly with this breakdown and the widespread suffering and unrest associated therewith, a revolutionary mass psychology will arise. Then will be the opportunity for those who for one reason or another, temperamental, economic, or educational, have acquired a socialist mentality under capitalism. They will seize the reins of power and will hold sway while the remoulding of social institutions is engendering a quasi-universal socialist mentality. But no group of bourgeois intellectuals can do this successfully, however much they may be fired with revolutionary zeal, or however clear-cut their notions of socialist reconstruction. The new political organism need not be, perhaps at first cannot be, " broad-based upon the people's will "; but it must be broad-based upon proletarian ideology; it must harmonise with instinctively felt proletarian needs; and it must in large measure be a spontaneous outgrowth of creative evolution or creative

PROLETARIAN DICTATORSHIP 135

revolution, which in this cycle of human history is operating through the conation, through the impulses and the desires, of the class-conscious proletariat. During the phase of dictatorship, the inefficient discipline that capitalism imposes from above will gradually be replaced, as it is being replaced in Russia to-day, by the efficient self-discipline of enlightened workers, fully comprehending the social character of production, and able to realise social solidarity in a way that is impossible in a society rent asunder by the class struggle. Gradually, as popular ideology is modified by the new conditions, the stringency of the dictatorship will relax, and the coordinations of the workers will come more and more to resemble the harmonious self-discipline of an orchestra or a choir ; while the dictatorship in its turn will become more like the guiding will and inspiration of a competent orchestral conductor or choirmaster.

Slowly and somewhat reluctantly have the present writers come to accept the views here set forth. In " The Plebs Magazine " for November, 1917, reviewing Karl Liebknecht's *Militarism and Antimilitarism*, they wrote : " We do not share Newbold's enthusiasm for the phrase ' the dictatorship of the proletariat.' To dictate is as repugnant to a truly civilised being as to be dictated to. ' Power, like a desolating pestilence ' . . ." Walton Newbold took up the gauntlet in the December " Plebs," enquiring pertinently enough what was our criterion of " civilisation." We replied in the same

136 CREATIVE REVOLUTION

magazine for January, 1918. Civilisation, we wrote, had two dominant characteristics : in the first place, force and compulsion tended to recede more and more into the background as civilisation advanced ; concomitantly, there was a growing hostility to exploitation, whether active or passive. We continued as follows : " As to the dictatorship of the proletariat, we do not think that there is any essential difference between your outlook and ours. We fully agree that the social revolution is going to be no matter of peace by negotiation, no pacifist pilgrimage into the promised land. But we think it probable that in that revolution the use of force will not be obtrusive. In the earlier stages, doubtless, of industrial unionist organisation, there will be numerous manifestations of force on the part of the authorities, and there will be numerous manifestations of what Sorel terms violence, i.e. of proletarian reaction against the authority of a class state. But by the time the workers are sufficiently well organised to expropriate the expropriators, their reserves of power will have become so enormous that the use of coercive methods will be needless—force will remain in the background. Be this forecast true or false, we cannot but feel that a dictatorship of the proletariat would involve the dangers of all dictatorships, the dangers that invariably wait upon absolute power. The difference in outlook is here largely verbal, but we dislike the brandishing of this particular phrase, not because of the effect we fear it may

PROLETARIAN DICTATORSHIP 137

have upon the bourgeois mind, but because it involves notions which are disharmonious with our general conception of civilisation."

This controversy took place in the, closing months of 1917, and we realise to-day that our " general conception of civilisation " was utopian, in the sense that it belongs to a development of civilisation that has not yet been realised, and cannot be realised until we have passed through dictatorship to ergatocracy—and beyond. Should any charge us with inconsistency, we shall reply in the bold phrase of Emerson : " Speak what you think now in hard words, and to-morrow speak what to-morrow thinks in hard words again, though it should contradict everything you said to-day." The bolshevik revolution occurred in November, 1917, and it has altered many outlooks, sending some rightward and some leftward. The issues brought to the front by the bolshevik revolution have convinced the present writers that the dictatorship of the proletariat is an indispensable phase in the revolutionary transition, and not for Russia alone. In conjunction with the tactic of the class struggle, and in opposition to the opportunism of the socialist parliamentarians, the doctrine and the tactic of proletarian dictatorship has become the touchstone of communist faith. Hence its outstanding position in the manifesto of the Third International. The Russian revolution, evolving the soviet as the most efficient revolutionary instrument, has further shown how, through the soviet, which

188   CREATIVE REVOLUTION

organises production during the period of transition to fully realised communism, there can
be also exercised with the minimum of danger
the inevitable dictatorship of the proletariat.

What is the history of the doctrine? It is
characteristically Marxist. In this connection,
as always when we quote Marx, it is not because
we believe Marx to be infallible, not because
we wish to stand in the shelter of a great name;
but because Marxism in action, Marxism re-
stated in view of twentieth century needs, has
been one of the main motive forces of the bolshevik revolution, and is one of the chief
inspirations of the revolutionary movement in
this and other western lands. Marx did not
foresee the soviet or workers' committee. That
is to-day's contribution of creative revolution.
But seventy years ago Marx foresaw that we
must pass through dictatorship on our way to
ergatocracy. Like nearly all Marx's teaching,
the doctrine is implicit in the Communist Manifesto, although the actual word "dictatorship"
is not used in that document. We read, however, that "veiled civil war . . . breaks out
into open revolution, and . . . the violent overthrow of the bourgeoisie lays the foundation
for the sway of the proletariat." Again: "The
immediate aim of the communists is . . . the
conquest of political power by the proletariat."
And again: "The first step in the revolution
by the working class is to raise the proletariat
to the position of ruling class." In his *Class
Struggles in France*, the history of the French

PROLETARIAN DICTATORSHIP 139

working-class movement from 1848 to 1850, published in the " New Rhenish Gazette " during 1850, Marx uses the word " dictatorship." The pusillanimous demands of the bourgeoisie were, he says, no longer of importance : " Now was heard the bold revolutionary battle-cry, ' Overthrow the bourgeoisie and establish the dictatorship of the working class ! ' " By 1875 the doctrine had been definitely formulated, for in his critique of the Gotha programme Marx wrote : " Between capitalist society and communist society lies the period of the revolutionary transformation of the one into the other. Correspondent with this there will be a period of political transformation during which the state can be nothing other than the revolutionary dictatorship of the proletariat." One more quotation must suffice to complete the account of the development of the theory. At Moscow, early in 1918, addressing the Central Executive Committee of the Soviets, Lenin said : " We pass from economic independence to labour self-discipline ; our power must be the power of labour. The dictatorship of the proletariat does not consist in the overthrow of the bourgeoisie and the landowners merely. . . . It has for its object the establishment of order, discipline, the productivity of labour, sound finance, and government by the proletarian soviet power which is much more stable and firmer than any previous form of government."

But why, it may be asked, is this transitional stage of dictatorship necessary ? Why cannot

140   CREATIVE REVOLUTION

we persuade demos, or persuade at least half of demos plus one, that our theories of social reconstruction are sound, and then peacefully vote the inauguration of the new era ? Why cannot we reach our goal by the tranquil process of evolutionary reform ? For no more and no less abstruse a reason than this, that man as an individual is not built that way, and human society does not work along the suggested lines. The point at issue between the communists of the Third International and the socialists of the Second International involves the whole conception of the nature of contemporary society, and this matter was discussed in the opening chapters. Parliament, on the democratic theory, is supposed to represent the collective will, and if it does not represent it, "it ought to." The democratic theory is that by informing the collective intelligence, and thus gradually modifying the collective will, we may modify its expression, parliament, and may in due time, with no more serious struggle than that of the advertisement hoardings and the electoral hustings, consummate what Newbold graphically terms our pacifist pilgrimage into the promised land. But if in its essential nature parliament be merely the expression of capitalist class rule, then the attempt to achieve communism through parliament is foredoomed to failure. That aspect of the question will be considered in the chapter on " Socialism Through Parliament or Soviet ? " Here we are not concerned with this mainly theoretical outlook. Even if we

PROLETARIAN DICTATORSHIP 141

grant the right-wing contention, it really amounts to no more than this; had social evolution taken another course, parliament might have been used as the means of instituting the co-operative commonwealth. We wish our friends joy of their might-have-been! Let us turn to the practical needs of the hour. No matter how useful a tool may be theoretically, it is in practice useless if the artist or artisan throws it aside and insists on using a tool more to his own taste. Such is the fate of parliament. It is futile to say that the workers could, an they would, expropriate the expropriators by the exercise of the parliamentary franchise. Ramsay Mac-Donald thinks they could ; we ourselves think the attempt would inevitably fail ; Hilaire Belloc believes that endeavours to buy and tax and legislate the capitalists out of existence will not lead to the cooperative commonwealth but to the servile state. But our respective opinions have nothing to do with the case, if the workers, if the class-conscious proletarians, if the members of the new working-class intelligentsia (who alone count in this connection), have made up their minds that parliament is the instrument of bourgeois domination, and that they will not waste time, money and energy in the attempt to use if for proletarian aims. This is a question of fact and not of theory ; a question of know-ledge of electoral statistics and of the working-class mind. Doubtless we shall differ from the right wing upon the facts no less than upon the theory, and here we must be content to record

142 CREATIVE REVOLUTION

our conviction that the whole movement of enlightened working-class opinion, the kind of opinion that will help to make history in the revolutionary situation that has issued from the war, is away from parliament and towards direct action. At most the class-conscious workers look upon parliament as a second string to their bow, and as a string that will certainly not save them in the battle should the first string fail.

But from another side we must return to the field of pure theory. What is the basis of the democratic theory of progress ? Is it not a belief that man is an essentially rational being ; the belief that the actions of the average man are guided by rational considerations ; the belief that by ratiocination you can effect a fundamental change in the goals towards which Tom, Dick, and Harry direct their respective energies ? The modern psychologist knows better. He knows that, broadly speaking, Tom, Dick, and Harry direct their course through life under the influence of subconscious urges, and that the chief use to which they put their intelligence is to rationalise to their own satisfaction all that they undertake. They find reasons for what they want to do. Within limits, they can be moulded by education during the plastic period of youth. In adult life they can be greatly influenced by revolutionary changes in the familiar environment—witness the revolutionary spirit that is abroad to-day. But they cannot, in the mass, be much affected by such arguments as are put before them in a parliamentary

PROLETARIAN DICTATORSHIP 143

campaign. When arguments are forthcoming ! Influenced they are, often enough, by emotional appeals masquerading as arguments. And it is by such emotional appeals, skilfully directed towards the ostensibly conflicting interests of the unclass-conscious proletarians, that our bourgeois oligarchs have played in the past and will continue to play in the future their time-honoured game of divide and rule.

It is only, therefore, by the dictatorship of a rival oligarchy, an oligarchy composed of the new proletarian intelligentsia, that the rule of the bourgeoisie can be definitively overthrown. The members of this new proletarian intelligentsia will be mainly driven, like other folk, by impulse and desire. But the impulse and desire have been created in them, in part by the economic circumstances of their lives, and in part by theory, socialist theory, acting on them during the formative years of early manhood and womanhood. It has filled their minds with the vision of a reconstructed society which shall at length be worthy of the name. It has inspired them with the unshakable conviction that when the economic developments leading to the break-up of capitalism have reached their climax, a revolutionary mass psychology will arise, and that upon them will it devolve to save the world from chaos by using that revolutionary mass psychology to revolutionary ends. Within the soviets, within the workers' committees, these members of the working-class intelligentsia will continue to labour, building up the new organisations, diffusing the new

144   CREATIVE REVOLUTION

ideas, animating the new wills, until the hour strikes. Then in Britain, in other lands of Western Europe, in America, and doubtless ere long in the far east, the new revolutionary instruments will, as in Russia, create the new political expression aptest for the new economic power of the proletariat. And here, as in Russia, dictatorship must infallibly be exercised in the initial stages, while the expropriators are being expropriated, while the power of the bourgeoisie is being permanently broken, while the economic stresses of the opening years are being overcome, and while the mentality of Tom, Dick, and Harry, of their wives and of their children, is being gradually adapted to the new order of society.

We who hold such opinions may of course be wrong. But we hold them, and we pursue our own ends guided by our own lights. We were feeling our way towards these opinions before August, 1914. " There is but one revolution that avails," wrote Ibsen. " It is, to revolutionise men's minds." To a Marxist, this seems no more than a partial truth ; but the war, revolutionising or rapidly changing economic conditions, has simultaneously revolutionised men's minds. Our views have been greatly clarified, our conative trends have been enormously stimulated, by the new perspectives opened out by the bolshevik revolution. Left-wing socialists have no use for parliamentary democracy. They are out for communist ergatocracy. And we of the Third International expect to achieve it by way of the Dictatorship of the Proletariat.

CHAPTER NINE

THE
IRON
LAW OF
OLIGARCHY

The Grand Lunar searched me with questions. " And for all sorts of work you have the same sort of man. But who thinks ? Who governs ? "—I gave him an outline of the democratic method.—When I had done he ordered cooling sprays upon his brow, and then requested me to repeat my explanation, conceiving something had 'miscarried.— . . . " But you said *all* men rule ? " he pressed.—" To a certain extent," I said, and made, I fear, a denser fog with my explanation.— He reached out to a salient fact. " Do you mean," he asked, " that there is no Grand Earthly ? "—I thought of several people, but assured him finally there was none.

H. G. WELLS.

CHAPTER NINE

THE IRON LAW OF OLIGARCHY

IT is not surprising that the Grand Lunar needed cooling sprays upon his brow after a vigorous attempt to understand the working of terrene democratic institutions! In the moon there was no problem of government. The ruler was ruler in virtue of biological specialisation. He had the largest and best-equipped brain in all his insect world. He was served by a hierarchy of large-brained subordinates. Down to the lowest gradations, each worker was biologically specialised, in body and brain alike, for the services he was peculiarly fitted to perform in the entomological community. But in the planet Terra *all* rule, for all are equally fitted to rule, and all desire to rule. At least that is the democratic theory —at election times. But in the later stages of the conversation with the Grand Lunar, Cavor was constrained to admit that though men had similar bodies and dressed alike, their minds differed, and they wanted to do different things. Herein lies the crux of democracy. It is impossible for all men to rule, for many men do not wish to rule ; many men have absolutely no interest in the problems of government or

148 CREATIVE REVOLUTION

administration. There is the fact, and what are we going to do about it ?

Look at the matter from a different aspect. In another of the most enthralling of his works, *A Modern Utopia*, the author of *The First Men in the Moon* suggests a classification of mankind, rough and ready, but extraordinarily enlightening. Men and women may, he says, broadly speaking be assigned to one or other of four varieties. They are (1) poietic or creative, or (2) kinetic or efficient, or (3) dull, or (4) base. Accepting this as an approximation to the truth, we have to draw the following conclusion. However much, by modifying the biological man through eugenic selection, and by modifying the social man through education (i.e. through changing the social environment), we may hope to reduce the proportion of the dull and the base, nevertheless with a rising standard of intelligence and character there will inevitably persist a notable percentage of the comparatively dull, and perhaps not a few of the comparatively base. And the distinction between the " artists," those who are predominantly poietic, and the " men or women of action," those who are predominantly kinetic, will, as far as we can foresee, endure to the end of time. Yet the democratic theory slurs all these differences in its attempt to realise the equal "right " of all citizens to rule.

It need hardly be pointed out that the whole drift of the present study is to emphasise the contention that, within the framework of the

THE IRON LAW OF OLIGARCHY 149

class state, democracy is a figment. Bourgeois democracy, at any rate, is no more than a means for securing the maintenance of ownership rule, what time the masses, the exploited, are led to believe themselves equal participators in the work of government. Even if we grant that many of the bourgeois oligarchs are self-deceived by their own ideology, that they are the slaves of their own formulas, this does not save us from the necessity of bringing about a forcible overthrow of their democratic rule. In the previous chapter it was shown that we must establish the dictatorship of the proletariat as a means of revolutionary transition. The centralised, class-ruled state of the bourgeoisie must, for the time being, be replaced by the centralised class-ruled state of the proletariat. That is the core of Marxist theory. That is the most conspicuous lesson of the Russian upheaval of 1917. That is the essence of what Lenin has to teach in his monograph on *The State and Revolution.* But afterwards, what will happen? Even supposing that to the government of men there succeeds the administration of things, even supposing that the state as we know it " dies out " or " withers away," shall we then achieve the proletarian democracy of which Lenin is fond of speaking? Shall we attain democracy in any intelligible sense of the term? Wells, in his utopian romance, foreshadows an aristocracy of intelligence. The world is to be run by a " samurai order," neither hereditary like the samurai caste

150   CREATIVE REVOLUTION

of feudal Japan, nor selected by competitive examination like the mandarin class of pre-revolutionary China. It is to be a " voluntary nobility," whose members will live by rule like any Trappist or Cistercian monk, will find in the discipline of their order the most congenial method of self-expression, and the means to fit themselves for the best possible performance of their chosen task—which is, to maintain and extend the conquest of man over nature, and to make Utopia a planet increasingly worth inhabiting. The masses, the dull and the base, though far less dull and base than persons to whom we must now give those names, will do their daily work and enjoy their daily amuse-ments, Gallios, as most men and women are to-day, caring for none of the things which so profoundly interest the samurai. This is one attempt, and a bold one, to face a problem which all must face who have realised the hollowness of democracy, and who are none the less convinced that a new order is coming for society, that we are entering upon a new era in man's conquest of nature. It must be faced by all those who want to help in that conquest, and to assist in the upbuilding of the cooperative commonwealth. There is no escape from what Robert Michels, in his *Political Parties*, terms " the iron law of oligarchy."

Not merely is the unworkableness of demo-cracy pointed out by friendly critics of the system like Michels and Ostrogorsky ; not merely is the criticism pressed home with relent-

THE IRON LAW OF OLIGARCHY 151

less severity by such declared defenders of class rule as W. H. Mallock ; but further, long before the war and the Russian revolution, perspicacious left-wing socialists were coming to realise that, to say the least of it, democracy might make for reaction quite as much as for progress, and they were, on this ground, advocating a frank acceptance of the oligarchical principle. Take, for example, the words of Edouard Berth ("Le Mouvement Socialiste," November 1, 1904), words which breathe enthusiasm for the policy of the strong hand in conjunction with profound admiration for the grandeur of the creative will. "The bourgeoisie has always looked upon the interest of its own class as identical with the national interest ; it has invariably regarded wealth in its own hands as equivalent to wealth in the hands of the nation. Such a view is very natural, for a vigorous and creative will always tends to look upon itself as a general will, boldly and yet legitimately confounding its own interest with the interest of the community at large." It is held, of course, by many syndicalists that all impulse to action must start from the masses, and that the syndicalist leaders are merely the exponents of this impulse. But if the philosophy of creative revolution which the present writers have adopted be sound, the revolutionary impulse does indeed come from the masses, but it is blind, and will lead only to ineffective revolt unless a sufficient minority exists fully aware of the end to be attained

152   CREATIVE REVOLUTION

and of the means of realisation, and prepared at all hazards to seize the favourable opportunity. Michels sums up the point pithily: " If they were logical, the syndicalists would draw the conclusion that the general movement of the modern proletariat must necessarily be the work of a minority of enlightened proletarians. But the democratic tendencies of our time prevent the formulation of such a conclusion, or at least prevent its frank avowal, for this would bring the syndicalists into open conflict with the very basis of democracy, and would force them to proclaim themselves, without circumlocution, partisans of an oligarchical system. The syndicalist oligarchy, it is true, would not consist (like that of the socialist party) in the dominion of the leaders over the masses, but in the dominion of a small fraction of the masses over the whole. There are a few theorists of syndicalism who already speak unreservedly of socialism as an evolution based upon working-class élites."

At least we are all agreed to-day—all who count for the purposes of this argument, all adherents of the Third International—that during revolutionary transition the stringent rule of a class-conscious minority will be essential. We must pass through dictatorship. The question is, what lies beyond ? Is it democracy or ergatocracy ? Or rather, is ergatocracy (for, whether the *word* become current or not, the *idea* of " workers' rule " underlies the whole foundation of contemporary left-wing socialism),

THE IRON LAW OF OLIGARCHY 153

is this ergatocracy which lies beyond dictatorship, to have a democratic or an oligarchical complexion? In a sense we talk utopia, for no one, however fertile in constructive imagination, can fully visualise the unknown future, can grasp all the magnificent possibilities of creative revolution. But we see in a glass darkly. And in that glass we see that the future organisation of society, the future system of administration, must commend itself to the general intelligence of a highly educated community. To that extent Lenin's " proletarian democracy " may come into its own, even though there will then exist neither bourgeoisie nor proletariat. Every caste system bears within itself the seeds of its own decay, and were the ergatocratic system the rule of a privileged caste, whether hereditary or appointed by competitive examination, whether aristocratic or bureaucratic, it would become enfeebled with the passage of the years, and would be overthrown in the end by the revolt of more lusty elements from beneath. Unless, in this restricted sense, the new order be " democratic," beyond question it will not endure. But fundamentally, none the less, we believe that communist administration will be oligarchical rather than democratic; and we believe that the oligarchy based upon ergatocracy will be free from the evils of the oligarchy of extant capitalist society, the oligarchy based upon bourgeois democracy.

What such critics as Michels and Mallock fail to see is that the whole conception of

154 CREATIVE REVOLUTION

oligarchy is modified by the social revolution. Mallock, doubtless, denies the possibility of the social revolution. He has spoken, it will be remembered, of "the buckjumping of labour," and the metaphor is significant of his views. He contends that production can only be carried on by the methods of the class state; that none but the bourgeois oligarchs or their henchmen can provide the requisite "directive ability." He makes much play with the failure of what he terms "socialist experiments," i.e. utopian communities founded within the framework of the capitalist state; but, in addition, he brings forward a whole series of theoretical arguments against the possibility of communism. Writing in November, 1917, he points to the Russian revolution as a striking example of the soundness of his theories. Two years later the suitable answer would seem to be the pragmatist's reply to the sophist's contention that Achilles could never overtake the tortoise. *Solvitur ambulando.* Which would you bet on in a walking match? Throughout the two intervening years, revolutionary socialists have been deriving fresh hope and encouragement from the great creative experiment of their Russian comrades. No one admits more frankly than the bolsheviks that they have not yet realised communism; but they tell us, and we see for ourselves, that the new Russia is the cooperative commonwealth in the making.

Let us imagine things carried a stage farther. Let us suppose, if not a communist world, at

THE IRON LAW OF OLIGARCHY 155

least a communist Europe, a European federation of soviet republics, including Soviet Russia. Would the organisation of these communities be democratic or oligarchical ? Without accepting in every detail the " voluntary nobility " scheme of *A Modern Utopia*, the present writers incline to agree with the H. G. Wells of 1905, that it will be mainly oligarchical. It will be oligarchical, not merely because the directive ability upon which Mallock lays so much stress is likely to remain a quality of quite exceptional individuals ; but, further, because the taste for the exercise of this faculty is far from widespread, and is confined to persons who are preeminently of the " kinetic " type, and who find in the exercise of these natural gifts the most agreeable form of self-expression. In the widest sphere of all, the sphere of social reconstruction, there is scope for the highest form of creative genius. Who can doubt that Trotsky is one of the most efficient army organisers that ever lived ; that this remarkable anti-militarist feels an abiding delight in the making and the management of the famous Red Army ? And who can doubt that Lenin and Buharin and the Lunacharskys are all persons who secure a supremely congenial mode of self-expression in their task of large-scale manipulation of man the social being ; in their work of modifying the plastic social environment, the very stuff and substance of which man the social being (as contrasted with man the biological type) is made. Fundamentally poietic, yet gifted

156 CREATIVE REVOLUTION

with a due share of the efficiency which the artist so often lacks, they are, before all, creative revolutionists.

After a generation or two, when the world has lived through the storms of this turbulent epoch, there may for a time be less opportunity for the activities of such titans of revolution. It may be, on the other hand, that in the field of social reconstruction, as in all the spheres of art, the acutely revolutionary phase will be succeeded by a prolonged epoch of unexampled blossoming. Possibly, however, mankind, realising for the first time the blessings of civilisation, will settle down to a period of repose ; to making the most, during decades of quiet content, of what has been achieved in years of almost unprecedented suffering. In that case there will be more need for persons of kinetic than for persons of poietic type ; and, whatever happens, the need for efficient organisers, for men and women specially gifted' in the matter of directive ability, can never pass away.

Let us take an extreme statement of that need. Mass power, declares Mallock, is illusory ; or rather, in so far as it exists, it is merely a capacity to obstruct or destroy, not a power to produce or create. " A nation cannot live by obstruction 'or destruction only. It can indulge itself in these processes for not more than brief and rarely recurring moments. Unless it is to die of anarchy, cold, and famine, its normal life-process must be one of continuous production and construction ; and as

THE IRON LAW OF OLIGARCHY 157

soon as any nation returns from destructive activities to constructive, the unlimited powers which are claimed for the mere force of numbers, as arrayed against authority external to themselves, disappear. The first thing which the masses of a people must do, when they are hoarse with proclaiming their freedom to do whatever they like, is to cringe to an authority which enforces on them the continuous production of food, and dictates the primary terms on which food can alone be produced. This authority is based on two things, against which a million wills are as powerless as the will of one : the first being the needs and structure of the human body ; the second being the constitution of nature, and in particular of the earth's surface. The primary business which is thus imposed on men, and from which there can never be more than brief intervals of cessation, is that of following the plough in good weather or bad, or bending over the spade or sickle. No popular will could abolish the business of agriculture, or radically change its character ; and if the power of the people is thus strictly limited in respect of the production of necessaries, it is limited no less stringently, though in part for a different reason, in respect of the production of superfluities. In proportion as nations experience the luxuries and comforts of civilisation, the things—things such as these— on which their keenest desires are concentrated, are things the production and multiplication of which are possible only through the action of

158   CREATIVE REVOLUTION

a knowledge and intellect which achieve an effective force in the persons of a few men only ; and it is only on condition that the people obey these few, that such superfluities can either be produced at all, or produced in sufficient volume to satisfy the appetites of the multitudes who are all clamouring for a share of them."

Achille Loria's sympathetic formulation of the same difficulty is in many ways preferable to Mallock's harsh and unsympathetic rendering. As far as material goods are concerned, the progress of civilisation, says the Italian economist in effect, has been dependent on the superior productivity of associated labour over unassociated. We agree, with one reservation. The evolution of the tool is likewise a fundamental factor of superior productivity ; and more efficient tools, once invented, become a part of the social armamentarium, misapplied to-day in production for profit, and to be rightly employed to-morrow in production for use. But the association of labour is vital. Hitherto it has been always effected by some form of external coercion : by the lash of the slave-driver ; by the power of the feudal baron ; and under the medieval guild system and under capitalism by compulsion which has been no less real because discreetly veiled. Under capitalism the coercive force has been wielded by the employer or his salaried manager, who represents embodied directive ability as far as there is a genuine need for that quality. The possibility of social-

THE IRON LAW OF OLIGARCHY 159

ism, real socialism as contrasted with the servile state (which, should capitalism break down, remains the only alternative if Hilaire Belloc's suggested return to a largely imaginary medievalism be ruled out of court as fantastic), depends on the possibility of the proletariat, through the soviet organisation, throwing up its own directive ability, and submitting to—not " cringing before "—that directive ability by a voluntary self-discipline which will replace the old coercion to associated labour. The discipline, to reiterate the image used in the previous chapter, will no longer be the discipline of the slave-gang or the capitalist factory ; it will be the discipline of the orchestra. If that self-discipline, that cheerful obedience to an oligarchy honestly organised from below, be impossible, then communist ergatocracy is impossible—and man's experiment in civilisation has failed. For capitalism is not civilisation, and no third possibility presents itself. Granted that the reorganisation of production is possible on the proposed lines, the system is, we contend, oligarchical rather than democratic, for it is based upon the preponderant ability of exceptional individuals, rather than upon mass rule. If our readers prefer to insist that an orchestra of volunteer musicians is a democracy, we will not dispute about terms. But it is not the kind of democracy which Cavor endeavoured to explain to the Grand Lunar.

As to " government," apart from the work of production, assuredly that too will remain

CREATIVE REVOLUTION

largely oligarchical. No one knows whether, after the revolutionary transition, the "rulers" of the ergatocratic community will be selected by delegation at two or three removes from workers' committees or soviets. It grows obvious that the main functions of the cooperative commonwealth will be economic; that as socialism is generalised, as exploitation within and without the nationally organised group passes into the limbo of an outworn past, the need for " rule " or " authority " as we know it in the class state will become increasingly rare. The state-as-power exists to-day mainly to defend property, exploiting capital, against the exploited class within, and against rival groups of exploiters without, exploiters organised as other national states. It is forced by the nature of its being to compete with other states for areas containing important raw materials, and for markets in lands where capitalist development is at a lower level. Hence the ferocity of capitalist rule, and hence the terrible instability of capitalist " peace." But under communism there will be no further need for these particular embodiments of the state-as-power, and therewith three-fourths of what we term government will have vanished from human ken. None the less, some need for centralised directive ability will remain. In this sense there will be scope for " politics," for the adjustment of numerous problems that inevitably demand communal solution when men and women are living together in a civilised

THE IRON LAW OF OLIGARCHY 161

community. From the very nature of human variability, the political organisation of the coming society will, in our view, be oligarchical rather than democratic. For the great majority will be, if not " dull," at least little interested in the working of the communal machine, provided only that it runs with a reasonable degree of smoothness and success. Once more, an élite, self-appointed like the " voluntary nobility " of H. G. Wells, delegated by soviets, or emerging in some way as yet unforeseen, will be requisite to ensure this reasonable degree of smoothness and success. But alike in industrial and in political life the perils of oligarchy will be minimised by the overthrow of capitalism, upon which the most disastrous features of the existing type of oligarchy depend. As for the period of revolutionary dictatorship, theory apart, Russian experiences already afford ample proof that the dangers of quasi-absolute rule are trifling if only that rule be exercised by those who have a clear vision of the possibilities of communist reconstruction, who are inaugurating a system the whole spirit and structure of which are antagonistic to caste, and who receive the unstinted support of the class-conscious proletariat. The " iron law of oligarchy " will remain in force ; but it will no longer operate to the detriment of the working masses, as it cannot fail to do while ownership rule endures.

CHAPTER TEN

SOCIALISM THROUGH PARLIAMENT OR SOVIET?

Parliament was on the one side a kind of watch-committee sitting to see that the interests of the upper classes took no hurt; and on the other side a sort of blind to delude the people into supposing that they had some share in the management of their own affairs. . . . Government was the law-courts, backed up by the executive, which handled the brute-force that the deluded people allowed them to use for their own purposes; I mean the army, navy, and police.

WILLIAM MORRIS.

You cannot stop a revolution, . . . although Ramsay Mac-Donald will try to at the last minute. Strikes and soviets. If these two habits once get hold, nothing will keep the work-men from them. And soviets, once started, must sooner or later come to supreme power.

NICOLAI LENIN.

CHAPTER TEN

SOCIALISM THROUGH PARLIAMENT OR SOVIET ?

IN the preceding chapters we have, by various roads, been led again and again to the same conclusion, that socialism, as we understand it, can only be brought about by a cataclysmic, a revolutionary change. Thus only can be effected a complete transformation of the social order, so that the words and the very ideas of master and servant, employer and employed, ruler and ruled, may become unmeaning. Thus only can be secured the complete overthrow of the capitalist wage system ; thus only can be shattered once and for all the power of the bourgeois state. We have now to discuss in fuller detail the reasons for the belief that it is futile to look to parliament and other democratic representative institutions as the instruments of this revolutionary change. Let us consider, first of all, the theoretical grounds why parliament cannot be of any use to the workers ; and then we shall pass to more practical reasons for the conviction that parliament and the extant machinery of local government will play no part in the revolution. Last of all we shall deal with the characteristics and potentialities of the soviet.

CREATIVE REVOLUTION

Why must the attempt to bring about socialism through the instrumentality of parliament necessarily fail ? For the following reasons. Throughout the history of the different forms of polity, each type of economic power has had its peculiar and appropriate method of political expression. The political activities of primitive communism were manifested through the folk-mote, or general assembly of the people. The city-states of classical Greece ; Rome during the days of her first expansion ; and the later Rome during the era of world-conquest, world-rule, and world-exploitation—each had a form of political expression suited to that particular type of slave state. Agrarian fendalism, with its serf peasants as the subject class and its barons and their retainers as the master class, had another political form. The medieval guilds secured their fullest political expression in the patriciates of the Swiss towns. With the rise of the economic power of the middle classes, a new form of political organisation has everywhere come into existence. Parliaments elected upon a territorial basis by universal suffrage are the ultimate expression of class rule in this form. Broadly speaking, the political history of the last three centuries has been the history of the perfectionment of parliamentary government as the political method by which the capitalist class asserts and maintains its dominance, against the feudal magnates it has overthrown, and against the new social type of wage slaves it has created.

But capitalism, and its political expression

PARLIAMENT OR SOVIET ? 167

parliamentarism, may well tremble, for the younger generation is knocking at the door. Another economic power is arising, the economic power of the workers, organising by new and up-to-dote methods. If we read the lesson of history aright, this new economic power will fashion its own form of political expression. It will not, probably it cannot, effect the overthrow of capitalism by capturing the political state as we know it to-day. It will not realise socialism through parliament.

Let us again make it perfectly clear that when we assert parliamentary action to be futile, we are not repudiating POLITICAL action. To do so would be absurd. By a natural, common, and unfortunate confusion of terms, " political action " is apt to be used as synonymous with " parliamentary action." For ten generations, parliamentary life has in Great Britain been the most conspicuous form of political activity. Just as to average persons of short views it seems that capitalism has always existed and will always exist, so also does it seem that parliamentary democracy is a perennial institution and the sole comprehensible method of political activity. Every Marxist student, nay, every competent student of history as expounded by capitalist historians, knows better ; but Marxists and competent students of history are not found wherever two or three are gathered together.

Yet wherever two or three are gathered together to pursue common life aims, and wherever

168 CREATIVE REVOLUTION

conflicting interests have to be harmonised, or, if irreconcilable, have to struggle for victory, there political action is born. The question for the revolutionary proletariat is : what form of political organisation, what method of political activity, will best favour the realisation of the growing economic power of the workers; what method will best hasten the overthrow of capitalism and the disappearance of the wage system ? The workers' committees' movement, the outgrowth of the shop stewards' movement, is inspired with a revolutionary aim; but some of those most active in promoting it, look upon it chiefly as a method for securing the control of industry. They concentrate attention upon its ECONOMIC aspect. But it has a wider, a POLITICAL significance. It is the basis of an entirely new method of political organisation ; it is the skeleton of the means by which the economic power of the workers will secure its new political expression.

Concomitantly with this development, parliament is proving itself incompetent even to discharge the functions for which it was created, it is proving incompetent to be the political expression of bourgeois class rule. Parliament exhibits progressive paralysis as the hour of revolution approaches. The battle, it seems, will be joined, not between parliament and the soviets, but between the executive, the inner cabinet and the permanent officials, the acknowledged executive committee of the capitalist class, on the one hand, and the workers organised

PARLIAMENT OR SOVIET ? 169

along the new lines, on the other. Parliament is so hopelessly effete that it hardly comes into the picture at all !

Here we pass from theory to practice. Parliament is so utterly effete that it CANNOT function as the instrument of revolution. The reasons for this have been fully explained in the eighth chapter. As far as parliament is concerned, the revolutionary workers are practising their favourite policy of " down tools." Attempts have been made in other lands, attempts will be made here by persons who still believe in parliamentary democracy, to adapt parliament to proletarian tastes and needs by such expedients as proportional representation, the referendum, and the recall—by the endeavour to infuse into parliamentary representation some tincture of that delegatory basis which to the proletarian mind seems essential. All such attempts will prove useless, for the workers are turning deliberately away from parliament, determined to secure their ends by another method, resolved to develop to the full the powers of that world-wide spontaneous growth, the soviet. The days of politics of the old kind are over. Under capitalism, the ostensible centre of political life has been parliament. But as the new era gets into its stride, as the foundations of ownership rule are gradually undermined, the basis of political life passes from ownership to industry, and political life can only find its true expression through the workers' councils or soviets.

" Under the existing regime," writes Lenin,

170   CREATIVE REVOLUTION

" whether feudal or ' democratic,' the ' people ' is really without power. . . . Inasmuch as all the power of a people is vested in its government, the people is divested of all power." But, he goes on to say (*Lessons of the Russian Revolution*, p. 28) : " the Russian revolution, now occupying the centre of the quaking world's stage, allows the careful observer to catch a glimpse of what that entity ' people ' really must be. The Russian people, struggling to assert itself, has in the travail of the revolution given birth to a new creation, flexible, mobile, and yet persistent as are the thought and will it expresses. This creation is the SOVIET." Again, referring to the origin and functions of the soviet, he writes : " In brief, these are the three phases passed through by the soviet, from birth to manhood : (1) it issued from the very heart of the people as GUARDIAN OF THE REVOLUTION ; (2) while growing, it served as the pendulum, the INTERPRETER OF THE REVOLUTION ; (3) fully matured, as the volitional and intellectual organ of its parent, it became the INSTRUMENT FOR REALISING THE ISSUES OF THE REVOLUTION."

Let us be perfectly clear as to what we mean by a soviet. Upon this point much disastrous confusionism still prevails. Look, for instance, at the " Daily Herald " for November 5, 1919. In this issue of our only labour daily, " One of the Victors," flushed with enthusiasm after his election as a borough councillor, gravely tells us that where there is a labour majority

PARLIAMENT OR SOVIET? 171

on a borough council, there you have a soviet. " Thinking of a soviet as a council of people who earn their living by useful toil, some of the new councils are in fact soviets. Especially may such a council as that of Poplar be considered a soviet, for all its members are workers except a very small minority." Could confusion be worse confounded? Of course the Poplar borough council, even with George Lansbury as mayor, will no more be a soviet than parliament with a labour majority will be an All-British Soviet, and no more than a cabinet with Henderson or Thomas as premier will be a soviet government. Yet Poplar, it will be contended, is a working-class district. The borough council has a labour majority. Why do we deem it ridiculous to term the Poplar council a soviet? To understand this we must know what a soviet really is.

The soviet in Russia is a council of workers' delegates. In this country the corresponding body is commonly known as a workers' committee. The name matters little, but the term " soviet " is concise; it lends itself to the formation of derivatives like " sovietist "; it has secured acceptance in all the languages of Europe, and it is used in all alike with the fairly precise significance now to be explained. It is a product of the new century: the work of creative evolution, the slower process, during the years preceding the war; and the work of creative revolution, the accelerated process of development, during the genetic era into which

172   CREATIVE REVOLUTION

the world entered upon August 4, 1914. " Genetic " is used here as practically synonymous with " revolutionary," for what process can be more revolutionary than birth ? Slow and gradual has been the growth of the parents, slow and gradual has been the fashioning of the embryonic life within the mother's womb ; but the birth of the child is a revolutionary outburst, birth is a triumph of creative revolution. The years since 1914 have been years of revolution, or years of revolutionary prelude, years of the lesser revolution to which a greater revolution will succeed in the near future. The years from 1914 to 1920 have not brought us socialism, but they have given birth to the parent of socialism, the soviet.

The soviet, then, is a council of workers' delegates. During the revolutionary crisis in Russia it was a council of workers' and soldiers' delegates. Obviously, the revolutionary soviet should have delegates from the army, the navy, and the air force, for soldiers, sailors, and airmen, armed workers, should be workers for, not against the revolution. But these thoroughly typical soviets cannot be organised in advance. They are, from their very nature, a product of the death-agony of capitalism. The basis of soviet representation is the WORKING GROUP, men and women *working together* in a particular place at a particular time. That basis differs fundamentally from the basis of representation to parliament or municipal council, which is the TERRITORIAL GROUP, composed of men and

PARLIAMENT OR SOVIET ?   173

women, indifferently workers and non-workers, *living together* in a particular locality at a particular time. It differs again fundamentally from the basis of trade-union representation, which is the TERRITORIAL GROUP OF CRAFT WORKERS. The last named offers at least this advantage over " democratic " representation to parliament or municipal council, that the individuals in the group are all workers ; but they do not all know one another, they do not all work together, and their organisation is not (as is that of the soviet) independent of craft or sex. It is not an economico-political organisation of the new type, based upon the realities of modern social production. Because the industrial unit which underlies the soviet is composed of people who meet daily as workers, the workers can thereby be effectively organised upon a class basis, and thus even under the capitalist harrow the soviet becomes astonishingly effective as a revolutionary tool. That is why we regard as reactionaries, and dangerous reactionaries, not merely those members of the possessing classes who, quite rightly from their own outlook, will use all the means at their disposal, all the forces of the capitalist state, to check the spread of sovietism. No less reactionary, no less dangerous to the working-class movement, are those socialists who continue to pin their faith to the antiquated bourgeois instrument of parliament and to ignore or frown upon the new proletarian instrument known as the soviet.

Let us now dwell for a moment on three other characteristics wherein soviet organisation is

174 CREATIVE REVOLUTION

radically different from parliamentary organisation. First of all, *the soviet authority is delegatory, not representative.* The primary group committees, workshop committee, factory committee, garage committee, building committee, dockyard committee, and so on (the whole organisation is being worked out by creative evolution here and now, to fit the facts and needs of British industrial life, and not in blind imitation of the Russian model), will send delegates to the local workers' committees. These will send delegates to the central committee of a more extended area, such as the extant London Central Council of Shop Stewards' and Workers' Committees. The intermediate committees will send delegates to the All-British Soviet. The delegates will go with definite mandates; they will be elected for a specified term, perhaps for three or six months; and they will be liable at any moment to recall. Further, and this is the second distinction of outstanding importance, the soviets will differ from parliament in that *they will combine executive with legislative functions.* They will carry out work in addition to deciding how it ought to be done. They will thus be continuously in touch with the realities of life, and will differ utterly from parliament, which legislates fitfully and ignorantly, and leaves the executive powers in the hands of a practically irresponsible cabinet and practically irresponsible permanent officials. Thirdly, whereas the inevitable, and proved, tendency of parliamentary rule is towards the maximum of centralisation, *the trend of soviet*

PARLIAMENT OR SOVIET? 175

rule will be largely in the direction of decentralisation. Hence the maximum of individual freedom possible to civilised man. To these three differential characteristics, a fourth may be superadded. Parliamentary government, the world over, becomes affected with progressive paralysis as the basis of social life is increasingly shifted towards self-conscious and self-governing industry; sovietism, on the other hand, as we learn from the practical experience of Russia, fulfils the pragmatic test—*it works.* Soviets express the revolutionary will of the class-conscious proletariat. Soviets, once started, must sooner or later come to supreme power.

We do not mean to imply that the whole scheme of soviet organisation can be worked out under the capitalist harrow. Nor do we venture to dogmatise as to the finished structure of the communist commonwealth. That must be elaborated in the future by creative evolution. For the moment we are in the revolutionary phase, and creative revolution is at work with the soviet. Not merely do the workers find in the group committees and workers' committees a means of self-expression which they can never find in the barren issues of infrequent parliamentary campaigns or in the sterilised activities of such democratically elected bodies as borough councils and boards of guardians; not merely are soviets the best organisations yet discovered for waging the daily warfare with the capitalist class; but further, in the decisive hour, when the revolutionary situation attains its climax, the soviets will be, as Russia

176   CREATIVE REVOLUTION

has shown, the best instruments for seizing political power and for enforcing the temporary dictatorship of the proletariat ; finally, when the expropriators have been expropriated, when " buckjumping labour " has successfully unseated his rider, it is upon the soviets that the revolutionary proletariat will depend for carrying on the necessary work of production. Here, too, a caveat must be entered against misunderstanding. We do not suggest that all the workers who are interested in the new type of organisation are inspired with a definite revolutionary aim. But they are aiming at something bigger than the immediate struggle for the standard of life. They are aiming at creative self-expression, and they are aiming at self-government in industry. Since self-government in industry is incompatible with the continued existence of capitalism, the soviet movement, as the capitalists realise, is essentially revolutionary, independently of the question whether the individual human units who make up the movement are consciously revolutionary or not. But as a matter of fact these units are consciously revolutionary to this extent, that they are no longer dumb, driven cattle, and that they are increasingly animated with a determination to refuse to run the machinery of production in the interest of an owning class. They demand effective control of the industrial process. They refuse to accept the semblance of control offered by the Whitley scheme. And the instrument they are fashioning for self-expression, for gaining control of industry, for

PARLIAMENT OR SOVIET ?   177

the carrying on of the class struggle on new and more intensive lines, is likewise the instrument wherein, as far as we can foresee, after the revolution the power of the workers will find its political embodiment. As regards the immediate future, there is an irreconcilable conflict of interests between wage-earners and owners, a conflict which bids fair to stop the capitalist machine before our present ruling class has had much more opportunity to display its genius for misgovernment. The breakdown nearly happened last October, as the outcome of the railway strike. It perhaps would have happened, owing to sympathetic extensions of that strike, had it not been for the compromising tactics of the parliamentarians. There is only one way in which that conflict of interests, that conflict of wills, can be brought to an end—by the expropriation of the expropriators and the final overthrow of the master class. Sovietists are convinced that " the buckjumping of labour " will be continued against any form of centralised statist socialism operating through parliament.

Altogether subsidiary is the question of abstentionism from parliamentary and municipal activity, upon which left-wing opinion, in Britain and elsewhere, is somewhat sharply divided. We are told that Rosa Luxemburg, during the last year of her life, never wavered, being always a convinced abstentionist. Karl Liebknecht, on the other hand, is reported to have said that every morning he rose from sleep an abstentionist, and that before nightfall the practical necessities of the political struggle always com-

12

178 CREATIVE REVOLUTION

pelled him to recognise the need for participation in the parliamentary campaign. The German Communist Party (Spartacus Group), of which the two comrades just named were among the leading spirits, has now been rent by internal dissensions, and those who differ from our own abstentionist policy assure us that Lenin is convinced that the impossibilism of the Spartacists, cutting them off from the realities of everyday life in Germany, is responsible for this disruption. Of course it is possible to hold, as many revolutionists hold, that every one who enters parliament is a soul lost to communism or perhaps a soul bought from it, and yet to advocate parliamentary and municipal electoral campaigning for propaganda purposes. Such would appear to be the meaning of the decision of the Independent Socialists of Germany, arrived at during the Leipzig congress in the beginning of December, 1919. By this decision, "parliamentary action is permitted only with a view to destroying the capitalist system, of which parliaments are a part."

It is often contended that the workers cannot afford to neglect any weapon in their struggle against capitalism. Does not this contention ignore the need for economy of effort on the part of those whose funds are scanty and numbers small? Persons who expect to achieve socialism by the conquest of parliament are, by hypothesis, right in attempting to win over the electors and to gain parliamentary seats. But those who consider that the social revolution must be brought about by a minority

PARLIAMENT OR SOVIET ? 179

prepared to take advantage of a revolutionary situation, ready to make the most of the existence of a revolutionary mass psychology, waste precious money and still more precious energy by tinkering with the bourgeois electoral machine. An abstentionist policy is no longer impossibilist for those who believe that the momentous hour is upon us. The call to arms has sounded, and we no longer have time in which to prepare and use all weapons. One who has the advantage of utilising a really up-to-date weapon of attack and defence, a Lewis gun, let us say, will be foolish if on the " any-and-all-weapons " theory he decides that he will also make use of knobsticks, assegais, and Dyak blowtubes. A man has but two hands. The revolutionary workers' best weapon in this country is not parliament, but the British equivalent of the soviet.

The stultifying effect, not merely of participating in the struggle on the parliamentary field, but even of holding any truck, where the class struggle is the issue, with the representatives of the bourgeois state, is admirably brought out by Robert Smillie in a frank acknowledgment made by him in the " Daily Herald " of December 2, 1919. Writing on " The Mines for the Nation " he refers to the coal industry commission, and continues : " The miners were very reluctant to submit their claims to a commission, for their previous experience of such bodies had led them to believe that commissions were usually appointed to get rid, for the time being, of some ugly question which it was not the intention of the government to deal

CREATIVE REVOLUTION

with seriously. Mr. Herbert Smith, Mr. Frank Hodges, and I were mainly responsible for the acceptance by the miners of the government's offer of a commission, and I can sincerely and honestly declare that had we not fully believed that the government would act on its findings we should have taken a very different course. We should have advised the men to reject the commission and to carry out the decision arrived at by ballot vote of the members of the Federation."

The extract speaks for itself. If you are making war, make war. The paradox of the class struggle is that even while it is in progress we have to live on terms with the enemy, to rub shoulders with them in the streets, to make a livelihood under the system in which they are the owning and employing class. But when the proletariat is using its massed forces to secure a vantage in the campaign, it should fight on ground of its own choosing and not on ground chosen by the enemy. The chains of capitalism are forged in the places where men and women work together. Capitalist dominion is economic, and parliament is merely the political instrument of bourgeois rule. We quote Rosa Luxemburg once again. "Where the chains of capitalism are forged, there must the chains be broken." It is by organisation in the key industries, and not by organisation in the parliamentary constituencies, that King Capital will be dethroned. "All power to the soviets!" was the watchword of the Russian revolutionists. "All power to the workers' committees!" must be the watchword of British labour.

CHAPTER ELEVEN

**CREATIVE
REVOLUTION**

How dare we expect that our eyes, whether of the body or of the soul, can be made to see more than they do see ? The objection is plausible, indeed serious, but it is met and refuted in experience. From the beginning of humanity there have been men whose peculiar office it has been to see, and to make other men see, that which without their aid would never have been discovered. They are the artists.

ALGOT RUHE.

. . . to explain what was the appeal of the [Russian] revolution to men like Colonel Robins and myself. . . . There was the feeling from which we could never escape, of the creative effort of the revolution. There was the thing that distinguishes the creative from other artists, the living, vivifying expression of something hitherto hidden in the consciousness of humanity.

ARTHUR RANSOME.

CHAPTER ELEVEN

CREATIVE REVOLUTION

THE words which Ruhe, the Swedish interpreter of Henri Bergson, writes concerning artists, that they are persons whose peculiar office it has been to see and to make others see that which without their aid would never have been discovered, contain a large measure of truth. If we think of artists in the narrower sense of the term, of poets and painters, of sculptors and architects, for instance, we are perhaps forced to accept even the amazing limitation involved in the use of the word "never." So individual is the work of the great artist that it remains for all time unique. Not twice will creative evolution, operating through the mind and the fingers of man, produce a Venus of Milo or a cathedral of Rheims. Not twice in the history of mankind will there live a Phidias, a Van Eyck, or a Dante, a Wren, or a Wagner.

But in the wider sense of the term "artist," philosophers and men of science are likewise artists. They, too, make us see that which, without their aid would not have been discovered so soon, and that which, without their aid, would perchance never have been seen so

184 CREATIVE REVOLUTION

clearly. Bertrand Russell, in his criticism of Bergson, complains that the latter's fundamental conception is not philosophy but poetry. Yet the very nature of the French philosopher's teaching renders him immune to the attack of his English colleague, for the essence of Bergsonism is that we shut our eyes to the import of philosophy if we limit it to the sphere of abstract reason. That is what makes Bergson at once so fascinating and so elusive to a generation trained to believe that for man the dry light of reason is the supreme guide to progress. From Bergson we learn that, in his view, a vital impetus, non-rational in character, is the driving force in evolution ; from Bergson we may certainly learn to recognise that, as far as human society is concerned, the dynamic of progress is as much in the realm of conation, in the realm of impulse and desire, as in the realm of " pure " intelligence—that figment of the metaphysicians in a world of tendentious endeavour ! Of Bergson, more in his proper place. Our point here is that philosophers and men of science are likewise artists in the sense of Ruhe, the Swedish Bergsonian.

Now among artists in this wider sense, those with whom we are chiefly concerned in our study of the dynamic of social progress are Newton, Darwin, Marx, Bergson, and Freud. Newton's theory of universal gravitation was one of the mainsprings of a movement which has dominated scientific thought down to the present day. Outside the range of science and

CREATIVE REVOLUTION 185

abstract philosophy, his chief interest would seem to have been the cultivation of a somewhat narrow religious formalism (he wrote for instance on the fulfilment of scriptural prophecy!); but his *Principia* greatly furthered the eighteenth and nineteenth century revival of materialism, the revival of conceptions of a universe in which the only "real" things are matter and motion. Towards such an outlook, under the influence of such philosophers as Aristotle and such poets as Lucretius, the classical world was tending prior to the barbarian invasion and the practical extinction of western thought which followed the triumph of ecclesiastical Christianity. With the acceptance of the doctrine of universal gravitation, materialism had a renewed and far more fruitful vogue. This phase was essential to human progress. It was necessary to exorcise the legion of demons, to rid the human mind of the plethora of imaginary "causes" which still lingered on into the eighteenth century as relics of medievalism. But it is no less necessary to-day to overthrow the new superstition which came to replace the spooks of demoniacal possession, to uproot the conviction that man is a thoroughly rational being and that the dynamic of social progress is a purely rational affair. If belief in witchcraft and similar absurdities be a belated survival from the dark ages, it is no less true that the hyper-rationalisation of human activities is a persistent relic of eighteenth century thought, of the ideas which were so preeminently

186   CREATIVE REVOLUTION

characteristic of the French encyclopedists. Diderot was doubtless justified in writing the witty parable conveyed in one of his *Pensées Philosophiques*. He imagined that a man, rendered misanthropic through betrayal by wife, friends, and children, retired into a cave to meditate some terrible revenge against the human race. At length, realising that it would suffice to bestow upon his fellow-mortals the curse from which they had hitherto been free, the curse of theology ; convinced that a belief in spooks would be a perpetual source of dread and misery ; he rushed forth from his retreat shouting " God ! God ! "—and his dread intent was fulfilled. But whilst, for certain scientific purposes, we shall continue to study nature and man from purely mechanical aspects, shall seek to learn all that we can from such an outlook as Lamettrie's upon *Man the Machine*, we can return, now that materialistic science has exorcised the spooks and demons, to the unbiassed consideration of man as thinking, feeling, and willing. We can recognise that the fundamental unit of human society is not man the machine, but man who is simultaneously machine and something more. Without any return to the dualism of the dark ages, we realise ever more clearly that consciousness (including, of course, what the Freudians term the " preconscious " and the " unconscious " spheres of the human mind) counts in human affairs just as much as, and perhaps more than, mechanism. Man is not merely a conscious automaton. For

CREATIVE REVOLUTION 187

man has what matter, as such, lacks. Man has sensation. And, as Bergson rightly insists, the function of a sensation is to call upon us to make a choice between an automatic reaction and other movements possible to us.

The work of Darwin marks a fresh stage in the achievements which have facilitated the modern outlook upon social life. Darwin may be regarded as the second of the great exorcists, Newton having been the first for the purposes of this argument, and with no thought of underrating the significance of the succession of noted names among the philosophers and men of science, the poets and the humanists, of the sixteenth and seventeenth centuries. Darwin compelled the realisation of the biological nature of man. Of little moment is it, in this connection, whether natural selection has been the sole or even the main cause of the evolution of man from a lower type. The outstanding fact is that, since Darwin, it has become absurd to question the general validity of the theory of evolution. Man is an animal, like other animals. He has become what he is through gradual growth ; and this conception applies to the human mind no less than to the human body. We will take the theory as accepted beyond dispute. The matter with which we have here to do is this. How does Darwinism bear upon our thought concerning the nature of human society, concerning the character, not of biological, but of social evolution ?

The first use made of Darwinism in sociology

188   CREATIVE REVOLUTION

and economics was to sustain the philosophy of exploitation. Social progress was conceived to result, like biological progress in general, from the survival of the fittest in the struggle for existence. Exploiting groups and classes, exploiting nationalities, were envisaged as successful types, predestined to effective perpetuation at the expense of the less successful types, the exploited. Modern criticism, however, has shown that even if it be true that the origin of species has been mainly the outcome of the Darwinian struggle, as far as the human race is concerned the biological analogy ceases to be operative from the moment when man becomes man. Human evolution is an artificial process. From the days when prehistoric man's brain-case attained its present size, from the days when the members of the primitive herds began to develop articulate speech and to turn their hands to the characteristically human occupation of toolmaking, men became to a preponderant degree exempt from the operation of the struggle for existence upon the biological plane. No longer had the human species to adapt itself to the conditions of existence. Men, beginning the unending conquest of nature, employed their accumulating knowledge in the modification of the natural environment to suit their own ends. Thus alone has it become possible for creatures so ill-equipped, biologically speaking, to spread over all lands and seas, to live in every clime, and of late even to challenge the supremacy of the natural deni-

CREATIVE REVOLUTION 189

zens of the water and of the air. Thus alone has it become possible for the poet to write without exaggeration : " Glory to man in the highest, for man is the master of things." To the distinction between the biological man and the social man we shall return ; but for the moment we are concerned with one of the latest and one of the greatest extensions of man's victorious campaign for the conquest of nature. As always, man has to conquer nature by understanding nature ; and from the conquest of the material world man passes through study to the conquest of that realm of nature which is itself in large part an artificial product—to the conquest of the social environment. The forces which drive man the biological animal and man the social animal are not for the moment under consideration. At present we have to consider man's knowledge of human society as revealed by one of the five supreme artists to whom reference has already been made. We come to the sociological theories of Karl Marx.

It is perhaps easier now than it was in the days of Pilate to answer the famous question, What is truth ? We would refer in some detail, did space permit, to a brilliant booklet, *The Criterion of Scientific Truth*, written a few years ago by George Shann. But the essence of Shann's criticism is pithily conveyed by Edward Jones in his *Papers on Psycho-Analysis*. " In the last analysis, the justification of every scientific generalisation is that it enables us to comprehend something that is otherwise obscure—

190   CREATIVE REVOLUTION

namely the relations between apparently dissimilar phenomena." This is the intellectual test of truth. Very different is the pragmatic test. The pragmatist asks, Does your alleged truth " work "—for otherwise I will have none of it. The great system known as Marxism, a system of economic and sociological criticism, with suggestions as to the dynamic of social reconstruction, answers both these tests. The labour theory of value and the doctrine of surplus value ; the doctrine and the tactic of the class struggle ; and the conception commonly known as the materialist conception of history (the theory that the mode of production in material life determines the general character of the social, political, and spiritual processes of life) ; this group of generalisations has enabled us to comprehend the obscure relationships between apparently dissimilar phenomena, and has contributed enormously to augment the dynamic of social progress. Marxism no less than Darwinism, will require modification and restatement as knowledge grows and as circumstances alter. Why, even as we write, Newtonism, the great generalisation anent the working of universal gravitation, a theory which had seemed to stand foursquare to all the winds that blow, is likely to suffer modification as a result of the hypotheses and investigations of Einstein. Truth is only true until it is superseded by a more comprehensive truth. But that supersession does not make truth into falsehood.

At this stage let us deal with a prevalent

CREATIVE REVOLUTION   191

misunderstanding of the doctrine of historical materialism. Though the doctrine was a manifestation of the general thought-trend we have been discussing, the thought-trend of which Newton and Darwin were such characteristic exponents, *historical* materialism is quite distinct from *philosophical* materialism. Historical materialism endeavours to explain the nature of social life during what Marx summed up as " the Asiatic, the ancient, the feudal, and the modern capitalist " epochs, as the resultant of the material conditions of production in these respective phases. He did not assert, as do the materialists in the philosophic meaning of the term, that the only " real " things in the universe are matter and motion. Nor did his doctrine involve a belief in determinism in the materialistic sense. It was not concerned with the general laws governing the origin and working of the human mind, but with the general laws creating opinion in the mass, under the conditions amid which men have lived in society throughout the phases just enumerated. The opinions of individuals are subject to individual variations ; but the opinions of the mass, said Marx in effect, are moulded by the dominant material conditions of production, and are modified from time to time as those conditions change. On the basis of this conception he analysed the working of contemporary capitalist society ; exposed the fatal contradictions inherent in the system of capitalist production ; and predicted that the downfall of bourgeois institutions was

192   CREATIVE REVOLUTION

at hand. The crisis arrived less speedily than Marx and Engels anticipated in 1848; but by the centenary of Marx's birth the soviet power had already been in existence for six months, and Marxist spectacles were no longer necessary to enable men to read the writing on the wall. Marx, we may recall, had long ago suggested that the great change was not unlikely to begin in Russia.

Utterly false is that conception of Marxism commonly put forward by superficial observers, that it reduces the entire content of history to an automatic process wherein the consciousness of the human units plays no part. In the first place, it is the human intellect in conjunction with man's impulses and emotional likings, and urged on by the spur of man's desire, which brings about the changes in the material methods of production. These changes constitute one of the most important parts of man's conquest of nature. In the second place, the material conditions of production react upon the mass psychology of society, arousing new tastes, generating fresh impulses and desires, modifying the intelligence, and thus leading to yet further advances. This interplay of material and mental causation which is the differential characteristic of human activity, is nowhere so conspicuous as in the process known as social evolution. Marx's "materialist conception of history" is a generalisation throwing a brilliant light upon the way in which the ideology of man the toolmaker is progressively modified as he applies the instru-

CREATIVE REVOLUTION 193

ments of his own invention. The point is one which previous sociologists had for the most part ignored ; and few but declared Marxists have even yet an elementary grasp of its significance. But the very last thing which Marx desired to convey was that what men think, what they feel, and what they will, have no influence upon human history, no bearing upon the average human lot.

Above all does the Marxist analysis of the contemporary phase of social evolution, the Marxist analysis of the nature of capitalist society, itself tend to accelerate the dynamic which is bringing that society to its doom. An advance peculiar to our age is that social evolution is becoming self-conscious, and this at one stride frees us from the absolute control of blind economic forces. The self-consciousness of the workers, their refusal to run society any longer as a profit-making machine operated in the interest of an owning class, is one of the principal causes of the break-up of the old order, and one of the main factors in the creation of the new. Capitalist production required educated workers ; nor has it been possible for the ingenuity of the dominant class to devise a system of education which will make the workers sufficiently intelligent for the purposes of capitalist production, and leave them with no inclination to look beyond the bourgeois ideology their masters would fain continue to impose on them. The socialisation of production while distribution remains individual-

13

194 CREATIVE REVOLUTION

ised, this and the many other contradictions inherent in the capitalist system, create the proletarian mentality and discipline the proletarian will. As the nemesis of capitalism approaches, these changes, following ever upon the rapid transformations in the material methods of production, create the framework upon which the new order will be fashioned. Nor is it necessary to assume, as do certain Marxists, that in accordance with some iron law of social evolution, the developments must take place in a predetermined and invariable succession. At this stage of human progress, the awareness of the end, and the revolutionary will to attain it, have become factors of equal importance with the development of the material conditions of production. Hence the marvel of the bolshevik revolution in Russia, a land where capitalism has hardly passed beyond its most elementary phase. Hence the communist developments in southern Mexico and Yucatan, superimposed upon the foundation of a peonage system even more primitive than the land system of Nicolaitan Russia.

The self-consciousness of the workers is now a vital part of the dynamic of social progress. This is at once the explanation and the justification of the tactic of the class struggle. Of course we communist ergatocrats are not (as the members of the possessing class, enmeshed in the confusions of their own ideology, are apt to declare and often enough to believe) agitators who create the class struggle. The class struggle

CREATIVE REVOLUTION 195

has been the warp and the woof of history athwart the ages from the days of primitive communism to our own. But we agitators certainly do our utmost to promote awareness of the class struggle, which the glib exponents of a fictitious social solidarity would fain conceal from the eyes of the under dogs. We know that when the workers come to realise, though but dimly, the essential nature of the system under which they live, the end of that system will be at hand, for then there will prevail a revolutionary mass psychology giving to a minority majority-power. The truly class-conscious proletariat, fully aware of the means and the end, will be able to assume the requisite dictatorship, and to pass through dictatorship to ergatocracy. The revolt of Spartacus, and similar slave revolts earlier and later, were no more than blind reactions of the oppressed against the oppressors. Similarly with the jacqueries of the serfs against the barons. Can we imagine a crowd of men and women like Spartacus and his fellows, a crowd of the associates of Wat Tyler and Jack Straw, meeting in a public place to discuss whether feudalism was better than chattel slavery ; whether bourgeois democracy was better than feudalism or than guild patriciate rule ; or whether (to use the new term) ergatocracy, based upon a soviet system, was better than all ? Doubtless from Piers Plowman and from folk-rhymes of the period, we can learn that among the working peasantry even at that early date there existed

196   CREATIVE REVOLUTION

a bemused vision of better things. But assuredly William Morris in *A Dream of John Ball*, retrospective with the vivid imagination of the artist, makes his fourteenth century peasants unduly reflective—just as Shakespeare, a man whose ideology was preeminently bourgeois, exaggerates from the other side in the picture of ergatocracy he incorporates in the caricature figure of Jack Cade : " There shall be in England seven halfpenny loaves sold for a penny : the three-hooped pot shall have ten hoops ; and I will make it felony to drink small beer : all the realm shall be in common ; and in Cheapside shall my palfrey go to grass. . . ." Cade might do worse ! He cannot now pasture his palfrey in Cheapside, for capitalism and the growth of population have destroyed the grass for miles round. But when he comes to power he will doubtless ease the housing problem for the time being by sharing out the mansions in Park Lane. Perchance in another matter, that of the small beer and the three-hooped pot, he will to-day follow the example of Lenin and Bela Kun, and eschew that of Kolchak the Supreme Ruler and Distiller of Vodka !

To the attentive reader who is familiar with the drift of Bergson's philosophy, it will we think already have become apparent why, in our series of artist-thinkers who incorporate and reinforce the new conception of social dynamic, the name of Bergson follows that of Marx's and precedes that of Freud. It matters little whether we accept Bergson's philosophy of the

CREATIVE REVOLUTION 197

élan vital for the realm of organic life in general, the vital impetus forcing an upward progress through the downward trending world of inorganic matter. Perhaps this is, as some declare, no more than the latest of the perennial attempts to sustain dualism in philosophy ; perchance it is one more shoot, artfully disguised, from what Robert Hessen has cleverly termed " the unhealthy root " (as opposed to the " healthy root ") of philosophy ; maybe, even, that, as Russell says, it is not philosophy at all but only poetry. Beyond question, it has strong affinities with the mysticism of Plotinus. But call it poetry, call it philosophy, or call it mysticism, no left-wing socialist who grasps the meaning of the vital impetus will contest the value of the conception (when applied to social evolution) as the obverse of the materialist conception of history. This idea of human conation, of human impulse and desire, acting and reacting on the material conditions of production, operating throughout history as the instrument of creative evolution, and manifesting itself in times of crisis as the quasi-omnipotent force of creative revolution—have we not here one of those generalisations which answers to the two great tests of scientific truth ; have we not here a truth which is the supplement and logical development of Marxism ? As far as the dynamic of social progress is concerned, the notion of creative revolution makes clear much that was previously obscure ; it fulfils the pragmatic canon ; it secures splendid verifi-

198 CREATIVE REVOLUTION

cation under our very eyes in bolshevik Russia. There, since November, 1917, we have seen creative revolution at work.

Enough, for the present, of Bergson. But why do we add Freud to the series ? What has the Viennese psychologist to do with the dynamic of social progress ? Already much, and he will have much more in the future—though as far as we are aware H. N. Brailsford is one of the few socialists in this country who has any glimmering of the fact. Whereas Bergson imagines that he has released the human spirit from the incubus of determinism, that he has restored the freedom of the human will, the psychoanalysers now enter the arena and produce abundant reasons for believing that we do not evade the grip of determinism by admitting the real validity of mental causation. Psychoanalysis shows that our most trifling acts are rigidly determined—nay, as Freud puts it, " over-determined "—upon the mental plane. Into all the reconsiderations, philosophical, psychological, and sociological, involved in this new idea of mental determinism, we cannot enter even in outline. Besides, the whole critique is still in its infancy. But one or two points must be considered, illustrative of the new lights Freudianism sheds upon the problems of revolutionary communism.

In the first place, Freud reinforces Bergson in the overthrow of the superstition that man is essentially a rational animal. When the spook of demoniacal possession (for the medieval doctrine of the soul was tantamount to a doctrine of demoniacal possession) had been exorcised,

CREATIVE REVOLUTION   199

two rival demons entered into the vacant dwelling, the demon of purely material causation and the demon of purely rationalised activity. The study of unconscious mentation puts an end to this new reign of demonology, while it simultaneously reinforces Marxist teaching anent bourgeois and proletarian ideology, and marvellously justifies the neo-Marxist or Plebeian contention of the value of tendentious education. Let us quote Ernest Jones once more. He refers to " the minimum of evidence often necessary to secure the acceptance of an idea that is in harmony with existing mental constellations, or to secure the rejection of one that is incompatible with these." Often enough, he says, emotional influences rather than reasoning, guide us, though all the while we imagine ourselves to be guided by purely rational considerations. The bearing of this upon the contrast between bourgeois ideology and proletarian ideology is obvious. No less obvious is it that the function of religious " dope " is to provide the un-class-conscious workers with an emotional or affective basis that will make them readily accept the ideology of the master class. In fact, while it is the popular belief that the will is the servant of reason, the truth is that reason always has been and always must be, to a very large extent, the handmaid of the will. But it is impossible here to do more than hint at the lights which the reconstruction of psychology on Freudian lines is likely to throw on the problems that face and the tasks that await the creative revolutionist.

200 CREATIVE REVOLUTION

In closing this brief and inadequate chapter, the merest outline of a theory of social progress which is being worked out amid the stresses and illuminations of an epoch at once more stressed and more illuminating than any previous age in human history, we have to add a sixth name to our list of creative artist-thinkers— the name of Nicolai Lenin. Quite recently Robert Williams declared that in the perspective of history Lenin would appear to be a much greater man than Marx, because Marx had been no more than a theoretician, whereas Lenin is a man of action. The comparison does not overrate Lenin, but it underrates Marx. Besides, we love not the device of the class-list. In Marx's day, the time for the man of action had not arrived, so we shall never know if Marx would have been as forceful a man of action as he was forceful in the field of world-shaking thought. Bakunin, Marx's great contemporary and his rival in the First International, spent much of a troubled lifetime in premature attempts to play the part of a man of action, and remained in consequence a pathetically ineffective figure. For Lenin was reserved the privilege of exercising his genius upon the plastic material of living humanity. Not because Lenin is the greater man, but because Lenin lives in a more stirring time, a time which Marx the revolutionary thinker has in no small measure helped to create, is Lenin able to find an artist's self-expression and to delight the artistic sensibilities of all true revolutionists, as archetype of the creative revolutionist in action.

CHAPTER TWELVE

FREEDOM

Many of the socialistic views I have come across seem to me to be tainted with ideas of authority, if not of actual compulsion. Of course authority and compulsion are out of the question. All association must be quite voluntary. It is only in voluntary associations that man is fine.

OSCAR WILDE.

Farewell Master ; farewell, farewell.
   No more dams I'le make for fish,
   Nor fetch firing, at requiring,
   Nor scrape trenchering, nor wash dish,
   Ban' ban' Cacalyban
   Has a new Master, get a new Man.
Freedome, high-day, high-day freedome, freedome
   high-day, freedome !

CALIBAN.

It is constantly forgotten that the destruction of the state involves also the destruction of democracy ; that the withering away of the state also means the withering away of democracy. Striving for socialism, we are convinced that it will develop further into communism, and, side by side with this, there will vanish all need for force, for the subjection of one man to another, of one section of society to another, since people will grow accustomed to observing the elementary conditions of social existence without force and without subjection.

NICOLAI LENIN.

CHAPTER TWELVE

FREEDOM

THE chairman of the people's commissaries of the Russian Socialist Federative Soviet Republic obviously regards freedom, rather than justice or some alternative abstraction, as the final aim of that remodelling of the plastic social environment which is the immediate purpose of creative revolution ; but he is under no illusions anent the possibility of dispensing with the use of force in the very near future. " We are not utopians," he tells us, " we do not indulge in dreams of how best to do away immediately with all management, with all subordination ; these are anarchist dreams based upon a want of understanding of the tasks of proletarian dictatorship. . . . There must be submission to the armed vanguard of all the exploited and labouring classes —to the proletariat." Thus the socialists of the left wing, libertarian in aim, are none the less authoritarian in immediate policy ; and this apparent contradiction is the main reason why they are regarded with such profound moral disapproval by another group of anarchising socialists, the champions of an ideal (and purely fictive) " democracy," who are fond of quoting

204   CREATIVE REVOLUTION

such liberal catchwords as that of John Bright the Quaker : " Force is not a remedy." In this concluding chapter, the merest note of interrogation, we shall endeavour, by an examination of the concept liberty, to throw some light upon the question at issue.

Dealey and Ward's *Textbook of Sociology*, an excellent work, which contains a summary of Lester F. Ward's notable contributions to sociological science, opens with an amazing statement. We read : " Man is not naturally a social being." The aggregative tendencies which human beings display to-day are declared to be a purely artificial product, the outcome of man's reasoned conviction that social life is advantageous. Ward here displays a confusionism unusual in so clear a thinker, but characteristic of the philosophical epoch to which he belonged. He was born in 1841 and died the year before the outbreak of the war. One of the first to realise the possibilities to be secured by the conscious direction of social evolution, he readily succumbed to the hyper-rationalising tendency of his day. Recognising that civilisation was an artificial product, that (as the present writers like to phrase it) the social man is an " artifact " almost independent of the Darwinian struggle, whereas the biological man is a natural growth like other animal species, Ward assumed that man's inclination to form social communities was an outcome of the reasoned calculation of a balance of pleasures and pains. Whilst it is true that human society is im-

FREEDOM 205

perfectly integrated when compared with such communities as those formed by the ant or the bee, so that the human being remains an individual in a much fuller sense than the term can be applied to the worker bee ; and whilst human beings have hitherto usually needed coercion to induce them to engage in associated labour ; none the less a study of human history and prehistory, coupled with the most elementary analysis of our conative trends, should suffice to convince us that man is by inborn characteristics a social being, contrasting strongly in this respect with egocentric biological types, such as the tiger. In non-social animals, gregariousness extends only to the family. A tigress will die for her cubs ; she will not die for another tigress. But just as the worker bee will die for the hive, so will a man die for the herd—for the " nation " or the " class." He will die for the liberation of Ireland, for the defence of Belgium against the Prussian, for an empire on which the sun never sets, for the advancement of the interests of the workers, " rationalising " his activities after the customary fashion. Stirner may tell him he is immolating himself for a spook, that in reality he exists for himself alone. But what Trotter terms " the herd instinct " is too strong for egocentric arguments. Man continues to yield to impulses and to find enjoyable self-expression in activities that satisfy the ends of man the social animal, impulses and activities that defy any rational calculus of individual pleasure-pain.

206   CREATIVE REVOLUTION

Yet all the while man, the arch-reasoner, sophisticates himself as to the motives that drive him to action ; explains himself to himself ; persistently rationalises his activities. You may study the process in detail in the mind you know, or ought to know, best ; or you may while away an hour reading Mark Twain's chief contribution to philosophy, *What is Man ?*

What is the bearing of these reflections upon the problem of freedom ? It is this. Should we accept the above analysis, we are constrained to admit that the anarchist notion of liberty is illusory. If man has a tribal self as well as an individual self, then freedom cannot be secured for the individual self alone. Shakespeare's Caliban typifies this truth. The poor drunken monster, primitive man infected with the vices of civilisation, even while chanting his hymn of freedom, his revolt against the slavery imposed by Prospero, turns to a new master, Trinculo the butler, a brave god who bears celestial liquor. Under a new master he will be a new man. So far only can Caliban advance towards freedom. The sole alternative he can find is the liberty of alcoholic intoxication—much as the American of our own day found that drink was " the shortest way out of Chicago."

We, at least, have got this far on the road to freedom. We have learned that freedom must be secured within the herd, and that it must be the accompaniment of civilisation. Scant as is the freedom of the modern wage-

FREEDOM 207

slave, he is freer than was his savage ancestor of a hundred generations back. In vain did Dryden make his hero sing :

I am free as Nature first made man,
Ere the base laws of servitude began,
When wild in woods the noble savage ran.

We know more about primitive man than was known in Dryden's day ; we know that it would have been truer to write " prone in the woods the cringing savage crept." The savage was not free from the herd, and no non-human herd imposes restraints more pitiless than those imposed by savage taboos. Freedom, as far as attainable to man, must be achieved through the best possible accommodation between the impulses and desires of man the Stirnerite ego, man the member of the family group, and man the member of the herd or social aggregate. No easy solution of the problem is likely to offer itself to the first comer, and hitherto the solution has been indefinitely retarded by the fact that the human herd has lost the simplicity of the prehuman phase, and has, throughout the history of civilisation, been split up into exploiting and exploited groups. But we shall not shuffle the problem out of the world merely by the abolition of exploitation. Treitschke does not hesitate to assure us that communism, which offers the highest conceivable degree of equality, involves in truth the highest conceivable degree of slavery, for it involves, he declares, " the suppression of all

CREATIVE REVOLUTION

natural inclinations." Yet all civilisation involves the suppression of natural inclinations, if by this term we mean those impulses of primitive man that are alien to the requirements of civilisation. The question is, which type of social organisation involves the largest number of desirable suppressions and the smallest number of undesirable suppressions. Communists believe that the system they advocate, substituting for distribution based on exploiting property and the wage system, distribution based on the free social satisfaction of all the primary needs (the sexual need excepted, unless by those who continue to believe that the bolsheviks have " communalised women ! "), would be an advance in the right direction. It would restrict what Russell terms the " possessive impulse," and would correspondingly favour the development of the creative impulse. The question is, how can we move along this road without finding ourselves permanently committed to the acceptance of the liberty-restricting activities of a new form of authoritarian state ?

Let us turn to consider the " suppression of natural inclinations " from the outlook of the new psychology ; let us turn to the Freudian theory of the unconscious. This unconscious, this Caliban in us, declare the psychoanalysers, sits unseen and for the most part unsuspected, directing the springs of action. It is the outcome of the repressions to which man, member of the civilised herd, has been ceaselessly sub-

FREEDOM 209

jected during the secular processes of that education whereby he is in each generation made over anew from the primitive which he is at birth, into the heir of all the ages of capitalist and precapitalist civilisation. The predominant characteristic of this uncanny monster is its dynamic trend ; unconscious processes are typically conative, say the Freudians, they are *wishes* ; it would perhaps be better to say that to a preponderant extent the unconscious is master of the *impulsive* life, for it seems more consonant with the ordinary use of language to talk of " unconscious impulses " than of " unconscious wishes "—but the connotations of everyday speech are among the many familiar things that will have to be reconsidered in the light of the new psychology. (This reconsideration will be a difficult matter, for—to quote Ruhe once more—" Language has not been built up in view of the need to convey fine shades in the changing colour of the inner states.") The unconscious is closely related to the primary instincts. " The unconscious," writes Edward Jones, " is the part of the mind that stands nearest to the crude instincts as they are inborn in us, and before they have been subjected to the refining influences of education. It is commonly not realised how extensive is the work performed by these influences, nor how violent is the internal conflict they provoke before they achieve their aim. Without them the individual would probably remain a selfish, jealous, impulsive, aggressive, dirty, immodest,

210 CREATIVE REVOLUTION

cruel, egocentric, and conceited animal, inconsiderate of the needs of others, and unmindful of the complicated social and ethical standards that go to make a civilised society. Yet according to the findings of psychoanalysis, the results of this refining process are rarely so perfect as is generally supposed; behind the veneer of civilisation there remains throughout life a buried mass of crude, primitive tendencies, always struggling for expression, and towards which the person tends to relapse whenever suitable opportunity is offered." Further traits of the unconscious self are that it is characterised by the immature and illogical mentality of the infant, i.e. of primitive man; and by the fact that its interests are predominantly, though not exclusively, sexual. Through education in the widest sense, through the environmental influences of civilised life, the primordial tendencies are repressed and much of their motive force is diverted to other, to social aims; from them is derived the greater part of the energy that animates conscious activities. Normally, much of the energy pertaining to the repressed trends of the unconscious is diverted to permissible, to social aims, a process known to the Freudian school as "sublimation." Wilfrid Lay, in *Man's Unconscious Conflict* (a recent work admirably fitted to serve as introduction to the study of the new psychology), sums up the meaning and uses of sublimation in the following words: ' The real causes of our daily behaviour having been revealed to us by psychoanalysis, we are

FREEDOM 211

in duty bound to reckon with them. When their symbolisms are understood by consciousness, a definite line of action has to be pursued in order to array the unlimited power of those unconscious wishes on the side of modern progressive social action. This process of enlisting the unconscious in the work that is available for social purposes is called sublimation because it sublimes (an old word in alchemy) or sublimates the crude desires of the unconscious. Just as the alchemists in the early days of science thought that they could transmute the baser metals into gold, so the philosophers have found that we can change the direction and object of the baser desires into higher ones having in them more gold—that is more value —for the modern development of society."

Only within the last ten or twelve years has Freudian psychology begun to force its way into the thought of the English-speaking world. Struggling against the conservatism of traditional opinion, it has been preached with picturesque exaggeration by some of its apostles. But new as it is, it has already surpassed the critical stage of homogeneity, and has split up into rival schools. Freudianism is destined to modify current outlooks as extensively as these outlooks have been modified by Darwinism and by Marxism. The three doctrines, supplemented in certain respects by Bergsonism, and building upon the foundations of materialistic science (summarised in the previous chapter as " Newtonism "), constitute essential parts of

212 CREATIVE REVOLUTION

the equipment of the modern mind. Without them, one and all, no adequate attempt can be made to approach a difficult sociological problem like that of freedom. Look at Lay himself, and note in the passage above quoted the blindness he displays when he writes of " progressive social action." Ignorant of Marxist criticism or ignoring it, he conceives of progressive social action as a simple undivided process, and speaks of " society " as if it were already a perfectly integrated organism. The unconscious conflict between Lay's hypothetical civilised man and the primitive " titan," the paleolithic Caliban who lives on within us all, is emblematic of the class conflict which permeates capitalist society. Society cannot be integrated until it has become fully aware of the class conflict ; nor until, when that conflict has been fought out and class has been for ever abolished, the titanic energies now absorbed in the class struggle have been sublimated to the higher social ends of the future. But as regards " individual liberty," does not the Freudian criticism come to reinforce the suggestions made in the earlier part of the present chapter, that liberty fully granted to man to-day, to man, proud man, as he stands in the foremost files of time, the product of centuries of Christian and capitalist civilisation, would be no more than the liberty of the drunken Caliban ? Man will continue to seek freedom and ensue it, but he is not born free. Everywhere in chains, the chains are not only those

FREEDOM 213

imposed by the authoritarian state. The chains of capitalist class rule have to be broken ; this is the workers' next step. Yet not thus alone, but through a prolonged novitiate, through self-discipline and increasing knowledge, will man achieve freedom. He must obtain freedom with a great sum, for he is not free-born.

Doubtless, as regards any proposed use of power or authority, the onus of proof always lies with the authoritarian. Just as in the matter of truth-speaking the civilised man cultivates the habit of telling the truth unless he has an adequate reason for saying the thing which is not, so the civilised man will cultivate the habit of renouncing the use of authority. Such compulsions as have to be enforced will be as far as possible indirect, and will mainly take the form " thou shalt not " rather than " thou shalt." In an advanced state of civilisation, even prohibitions will exist solely to remind us of things which we do not really want to do, but which we might do by inadvertence. Thus, after the solution of the class conflict, and after the transitional phase of dictatorship, man may hope to attain a large measure of freedom.

We are " free " when we need not submit to any constraint imposed by an alien will—when we can do what we like and like what we do. Note that we do not feel the restraint enforced by material conditions as impairing freedom to anything like the same extent as we feel the restraint imposed by another conscious being (operating, of course, through material con-

214   CREATIVE REVOLUTION

ditions).   We master material conditions when we can, and submit unrepiningly for the most part when material conditions are too strong for us ; but the coercion that issues from another's will arouses rebellion. The supreme objects of education and social organisation must therefore be to reduce to the utmost the conflict of wills.   Society must be so transmuted that the conflict of wills dependent upon class conflicts and sex conflicts, and upon differences between crabbed age and youth, may be as far as possible removed.   No "ideal" of social solidarity or sex solidarity will put an end to conflict so long as relationships of economic mastery and dependence subsist between classes or between sexes.   When these basic differences have been eliminated, the aim of education in the ergatocratic state will be, with a minimal suppression of healthy individuality, to produce the type of adult who will as by second nature desire to do what it is advantageous to "society" that he or she should do. Since man is instinctively social, the task will be comparatively easy when the contradictions that prevail throughout existing society have been overcome. Libertarian education, as practised in Montessori schools, as described in Faria's *A New School in Belgium*, as inaugurated by the Lunacharskys in the schools of Soviet Russia, aims at producing a thoroughly social human being, not by drill, but by knowledge and self-discipline. In such a being, the energies of the unconscious "titan" will be successfully

FREEDOM 215

sublimated, and man's unconscious conflict will to a great extent become a thing of the past. In like manner, human society will then be integrated for the first time since the dawn of civilisation.

To-day education in general, like moral teaching and religious teaching in particular, is utterly falsified by the habitual concealment of the class struggle. Not that we want to teach the class struggle to children, but it permeates the social world in which they have to live, as they will find out for themselves in due time. The repression of the class-struggle aspect of life and history, the pretence (necessary to bourgeois ideology) that there is no class struggle but a real social solidarity, lead, like other repressions and pretences, to profound mental conflicts in the realm of the unconscious, and to consequent disorder of the affective life.

We shall not, in the future society, escape the controversy between the statism of those who hold Hegelian and Treitschkean views of social life, and the egocentrism of Stirner and the latter-day exponents of anarchist individualism. Stirner, in truth, should not be regarded simply as an egocentric. He was something much more significant, for he was one of the great exorcists. In a complex society there will always be room for temperamental anarchists. If the dangers of statism are to be successfully and enduringly averted, anarchist criticism must never cease. But anarchism may itself become a spook. The solution of the problem, like

216 CREATIVE REVOLUTION

that of so many others, is really educational. It has now become possible to state it clearly, and a problem clearly stated is a problem half solved. We desire to produce an individuality which, when adult, is so thoroughly "civilised" that it has no effective desire for activities that conflict with the equal rights of others; that LIKES to be civilised, and yet has not had a pattern stamp impressed upon it; that retains with undiminished force the individual will to resist most strenuously when any outside ego, or outside corporative ego (state or other), attempts to ride rough-shod over the primary ego's own civilised self-assertions. This compromise between conformity and individuality is far from easy to secure, and it cannot be secured at all within the framework of the extant class state. Hence the first step towards the reform of education, using the term education in the widest possible sense to embrace all the environmental influences that act upon the individual, must be to smash the framework of the existing state. Commenting on Marx's *Eighteenth Brumaire of Louis Bonaparte*, and echoing the thousand-year-old phrase of Omar the anarchist, Lenin tells us that all former revolutions helped to perfect the machinery of government, whereas now we must shatter it, break it to pieces. Then only can we hope to remould it nearer to the heart's desire. Thus shall we fulfil our creative impulse, for, as Bakunin wrote in 1842: "We must trust in the undying spirit, which destroys and anni-

FREEDOM 217

hilates solely because it is the inscrutable and perennially creative wellspring of life. The impulse to destroy is likewise the impulse to create."

We return, therefore, in the end, to the conception of freedom which has inspired us throughout the writing of this book. We return to the idea that the revolution is a transcendent creative act, wherein man's will, guided by accumulating knowledge, asserts its freedom, widening the bounds of freedom alike for the individual and for the race. Does this outlook fail to deserve the name of philosophy? Does it belong, rather, to the realm of poetry? So be it. But let us never forget that "poets are the hierophants of an unapprehended inspiration; the mirrors of the gigantic shadows which futurity casts upon the present; the words which express what they understand not; the trumpets which sing to battle and feel not what they inspire; the influence which is moved not but moves."

" Life as a whole," writes Bergson (*Creative Evolution*, p. 284), " from the initial impulsion that thrust it into the world, appears as a wave which rises, and which is opposed by the descending movement of matter. On the greater part of its surface, at different heights, the current is converted by matter into a vortex. At one point alone it passes freely, dragging with it the obstacle which weighs on its progress but does not arrest it. At that point is humanity; it is our privileged situation." This eloquent

218 CREATIVE REVOLUTION

passage has but one flaw, its question-begging reference to the "initial impulsion" that is alleged to have "thrust" life into the world. Let that pass. What concerns us here is not the origin of life, but the vital impetus as it manifests itself in mankind to-day. Human freedom, with all its inevitable limitations, is precisely one of those phenomena wherein is displayed the triumph of life over material causation. We grant for purposes of argumentative discussion that this may be but another example of what Hamon has boldly termed "the universal illusion of freewill." Nevertheless, having exorcised the anthropomorphic spook from inanimate nature, having slaughtered the god of our own creation, we continue irresistibly to believe that our own will is the one "real cause" in the world! The will-to-revolution is for us the real cause of the creative revolution now in progress, a revolution that will signalise an enormous advance in man's movement towards freedom. If this be no more than poetry, we say with the poet : " Yet freedom, yet, thy banner, torn but flying, streams like the thunderstorm AGAINST THE WIND."

BIBLIOGRAPHY

I

BOOKS

ALLSOPP, HENRY, An Introduction to English Industrial History, Bell, London, 1912.

BACON, ADMIRAL SIR REGINALD, The Dover Patrol, 1915–1917, 2 vols., Hutchinson, 1919.

BELLOC, HILAIRE, The Servile State, Foulis, London, 1913.

BERGSON, HENRI, Creative Evolution, translated from the French by Arthur Mitchell, Macmillan, London, 1911.

BOUDIN, LOUIS B., Socialism and War, New Review Publishing Association, New York, 1916.

BRAILSFORD, HENRY NOEL, A League of Nations, Headley, London, 1917.

CARPENTER, EDWARD, Towards Democracy, Allen & Unwin, London, reprinted 1905.

CARR, HERBERT WILDON, Henri Bergson, Jack, London, 1919.

CARR, HERBERT WILDON, The Philosophy of Change, Macmillan, London, 1914.

COLE, G. D. H., Self-Government in Industry, Bell, London, 1917.

COLE, G. D. H., and MELLOR, W., The Meaning of Industrial Freedom, Allen & Unwin, London, 1918.

DANNENBERG, KARL, Karl Marx, etc., Radical Review Publishing Association, New York, 1918.

DARWIN, CHARLES, The Origin of Species, and other works.

DEALEY, JAMES QUAYLE, and WARD, LESTER FRANK, A Textbook of Sociology, Macmillan, London, 1905.

DIDEROT, DENYS, Pensées philosophiques [Philosophical Meditations].

DRYDEN, JOHN, The Conquest of Granada.

ENGELS, FRIEDRICH, see Marx, Karl.

FARIA DE VASCONCELLOS, A., A New School in Belgium, translated from the French by Eden and Cedar Paul, Harrap, London, 1919.

FREUD, SIEGMUND, The Interpretation of Dreams, translated by A. A. Brill, Allen & Unwin, London, 1913.

FREUD, SIEGMUND, Psychopathology of Everyday Life, translated by A. A. Brill, Fisher Unwin, London, 1914.

220 CREATIVE REVOLUTION

FREUD, SIEGMUND, Wit and its Relation to the Unconscious, translated by A. A. Brill, Fisher Unwin, London, 1916.

HAMON, AUGUSTIN, Lessons of the World War, Fisher Unwin, London, 1918.

HAMON, AUGUSTIN, The Universal Illusion of Free Will, University Press, London, 1899.

HARDY, THOMAS, The Dynasts, Macmillan, London, reprinted 1915.

HESSEN, ROBERT, Die Philosophie der Kraft [The Philosophy of Power], Hoffmann, Stuttgart, 1913.

JONES, EDWARD, Papers on Psycho-Analysis, Ballière, London, 1918.

JUNG, C. G., Psychology of the Unconscious, translated from the German by Beatrice M. Hinkle, Moffat, New York, 1916, and other works.

KIDD, BENJAMIN, The Science of Power, Methuen, London, 1918.

LAMETTRIE, JULIEN OFFROY DE, L'Homme machine, Leyden, 1748 (burned by order of the town council immediately on publication! An English translation, Man a Machine, was published in London in 1750).

LAY, WILFRID, Man's Unconscious Conflict, a popular exposition of psycho-analysis, Kegan Paul, London, 1919.

LENIN, NICOLAI, The State and Revolution, British Socialist Party and Socialist Labour Press, 1919.

LIEBKNECHT, KARL, Militarism and Anti-Militarism, translated from the German by A. Sirnis, Socialist Labour Press, Glasgow, 1917.

LORIA, ACHILLE, Economic Foundations of Society, translated from the French by Lindley M. Keasbey, Allen & Unwin, London, reprinted 1910.

LORIA, ACHILLE, Karl Marx, translated from the Italian by Eden and Cedar Paul, Allen & Unwin, London, 1920.

LORIA, ACHILLE, The Economic Synthesis, translated from the . Italian by Eden and Cedar Paul, Allen & Unwin, London, 1914.

LOWELL, JAMES RUSSELL, The Biglow Papers.

MACDONALD, J. RAMSAY, Parliament and Revolution, National Labour Press, London, 1919, and other works.

MALLOCK, WILLIAM HURRELL, The Limits of Pure Democracy, Chapman & Hall, London, 1917, and other works.

MARX, KARL, The Eighteenth Brumaire of Louis Bonaparte, translated by Daniel de Leon, 3rd edition, Kerr, Chicago, 1913.

MARX, KARL, Die Klassenkämpfe in Frankreich, 1848 bis 1850 (reprinted from the New Rhenish Gazette, Hamburg, 1850), with a preface by Friedrich Engels [Class Struggles in France, 1848–1850], Vorwaerts, Berlin, 1895.

BIBLIOGRAPHY 221

MARX, KARL, The Civil War in France [1871] with an introduction by Friedrich Engels, translated from the German by E. Belfort Bax, Kerr, Chicago.

MARX, KARL, Capital, and other works.

MASARYK, THOMAS GARRIGUE, The Spirit of Russia, translated from the German by Eden and Cedar Paul, 2 vols., Allen & Unwin, London, 1919.

MICHELS, ROBERT, Political Parties, a sociological study of the oligarchical tendencies of modern democracy, translated from the Italian by Eden and Cedar Paul, Jarrold, London, 1915.

MONTESSORI, MARIA, Dr. Montessori's Own Handbook, Heinemann, London, 1914, and other works.

MORRIS, WILLIAM, A Dream of John Ball, Longmans, London.

MORRIS, WILLIAM, News from Nowhere, Longmans, London, reprinted 1918.

NEWBOLD, J. T. WALTON, How Europe armed for War, 1871–1914, Blackfriars Press, London, 1916.

NEWTON, ISAAC, Principia.

OECHSLI, W., History of Switzerland, translated from the German by Eden and Cedar Paul, Cambridge University Press, in the press.

OSTROGORSKY, M. Y., Democracy and the Organisation of Political Parties, translated from the French by F. Clarke, 2 vols., Macmillan, London, 1902.

PATAUD, EMILE, and POUGET, EMILE, Syndicalism and the Cooperative Commonwealth (How we shall bring about the Revolution), translated from the French, Oxford, 1913.

RANSOME, ARTHUR, Six Weeks in Russia in 1919, Allen & Unwin, London, 1919.

READE, WILLIAM WINWOOD, The Martyrdom of Man, Trübner, London, 1884.

ROUSSEAU, JEAN JACQUES, The Social Contract, translated with introduction by G. D. H. Cole, Dent, Everyman's Library.

RUHE, ALGOT, Henri Bergson, Macmillan, London, 1914.

RUSSELL, BERTRAND, Principles of Social Reconstruction, Allen & Unwin, London, 1916.

RUSSELL, BERTRAND, Roads to Freedom, Allen & Unwin, London, 1918.

SHANN, GEORGE, The Criterion of Scientific Truth, Cassell, London, 1902.

SHELLEY, PERCY BYSSHE, A Defence of Poetry (selected prose works), Watts, London, 1915.

STIRNER, MAX, The Ego and His Own, translated from the German by Steren Byington, Fifield, London, 1915.

222 CREATIVE REVOLUTION

TREITSCHKE, HEINRICH VON, Freedom (Treitschke, His Life, and Works), Jarrold and Allen & Unwin, London, 1914.

TROTSKY, LEON, The History of the Russian Revolution to Brest–Litovsk, Allen & Unwin, London, 1919.

TROTTER, W., Instincts of the Herd in Peace and War, Fisher Unwin, London, 1916.

TWAIN, MARK, What is Man ? and other essays, Chatto, London, 1919,

WARD, LESTER FRANK, Dynamic Sociology, Appleton, New York, 1907.

WARD, see Dealey. and Ward.

WELLS, HERBERT GEORGE, A Modern Utopia, Chapman & Hall, London, 1905.

WELLS, HERBERT GEORGE, The First Men in the Moon, Newnes, London, 1901.

WHITMAN, WALT, Songs of Insurrection (Leaves of Grass).

WILDE, OSCAR, The Soul of Man under Socialism, Humphreys, London, 1912.

II

PAMPHLETS

Abbreviations :

B.S.P.—British Socialist Party, 21A Maiden Lane, Strand, W.C. 2.

I.L.P.—Independent Labour Party, 8 and 9 Johnson's Court, Fleet Street, E.C. 4.

L.W.C.—London Workers' Committee, 10 Tudor Street, E.C. 4.

N.G.L.—National Guilds' League, 17 Acacia Road, N.W. 8.

N.L.P.—National Labour Press, 8 and 9 Johnson's Court, Fleet Street, E.C. 4.

P.L.—Plebs League, 11A Penywern Road, Earl's Court, S.W. 5.

P.R.I.B.—People's Russian Information Bureau, 152 Fleet Street, E.C. 4.

S.I.R.B.—Socialist Information and Research Bureau, 196 St. Vincent Street, Glasgow.

S.W.C.—Scottish Workers' Committee, 31 North Frederick Street, Glasgow.

S.W.S.S.—South Wales Socialist Society, 38 Cemetery Road, Porth, Rhondda Valley, South Wales.

W.S.F.—Workers' Socialist Federation, 400 Old Ford Road, Bow, E. 3.

CAMPBELL, J. R., see Gallacher.

ENGELS, FRIEDRICH, The Development of Socialism from Utopia to Science, translated from the German by Daniel de Leon, S.L.P.

BIBLIOGRAPHY 223

ENGELS, FRIEDRICH, Revolutionary Tactics, translated from the German by Eden and Cedar Paul. (This is the preface to the 1895 edition of Marx's Class Struggles in France). In the press.

ENGELS, *see* Marx, Karl.

GALLACHER, WILLIAM, and CAMPBELL, J. R., Direct Action, an outline of workshop and social organisation, S.W.C.

GRUMBACH, S., Der Irrtum von Zimmerwald-Kiental [The Error of Zimmerwald-Kiental], Berne, 1916.

KAUTSKY, KARL, The Dictatorship of the Proletariat.

LENIN, NICOLAI, Lessons of the Russian Revolution, B.S.P.

LENIN, NICOLAI, The Chief Task of Our Times, W.S.F.

LENIN, NICOLAI, The Land Revolution in Russia, I.L.P.

LENIN, NICOLAI, The Soviets at Work, S.I.R.B.

LENIN and ZINOVIEV, Sozialismus und der Krieg [Socialism and the War], Berne, 1915.

LEON, DANIEL DE, The Preamble of the Industrial Workers of the World, S.L.P.

LUXEMBURG, ROSA, Revolutionary Socialism in Action, translated from the German with a prefatory memoir by Eden and Cedar Paul, S.W.C. In the press.

MARX, KARL, The Socialist Programme (Marx's criticism of the Gotha Programme), translated from the German by Eden and Cedar Paul, S.L.P.

MARX, KARL, and ENGELS, FRIEDRICH, Manifesto of the Communist Party, Reeves, London.

NEWBOLD, J. T. WALTON, Bankers, Bondholders, and Bolsheviks, I.L.P.

NEWBOLD, J. T. WALTON, Capitalism and the Counter Revolution, W.S.F.

NEWBOLD, J. T. WALTON, Marx and Modern Capitalism, B.S.P.

NEWBOLD, J. T. WALTON, The Politics of Capitalism, B.S.P.

PAUL, WILLIAM, The New Communist Manifesto of the Third International, S.L.P.

PRICE, M. PHILIPS, Capitalist Europe and Socialist Russia, B.S.P.

PRICE, M. PHILIPS, The Origin and Growth of the Russian Soviets, P.R.I.B.

RADEK, KARL, The Development of Socialism from Science to Action, S.L.P.

REED, JOHN, Red Russia, two parts, W.S.F.

RICKMAN, JOHN, An Eye Witness from Russia, P.R.I.B.

RUSSELL, BERTRAND, The Philosophy of Bergson, Cambridge, 1914.

STAVENHAGEN, C. H., Labour's Final Weapon, Industrial Unionism, printed for the author by the N.L.P.

TROTSKY, LEON, War or Revolution, S.L.P.

224 CREATIVE REVOLUTION

ZETKIN, KLARA, Through Dictatorship to Democracy, translated from the German with a foreword by Eden and Cedar Paul, S.L.P.
ZINOVIEV, *see* Lenin and Zinoviev.

The Russian Soviet Constitution, P.R.I.B.

The Miners' Next Step, issued by the Unofficial Reform Committee, Tonypandy, 1912.
Industrial Democracy for Miners, S.W.S.S., 1919.

National Guilds : an Appeal to Trade Unionists, N.G.L.
The Guild Idea, an Appeal to the Public, N.G.L.
Towards a Miners' Guild, N.G.L.
Towards a National Railway Guild, N.G.L.
A Catechism of National Guilds, N.G.L.
A Short Statement of Principles and Objects, N.G.L.

What Does Education Mean to the Workers ? P.L.

III

NEWSPAPERS AND MISCELLANEOUS

Files of the following periodicals :

DEUTSCHE JAHRBÜCHER FÜR WISSENSCHAFT UND KUNST (Jules Elysard [Michail Bakunin] Die Reaktion in Deutschland [Reaction in Germany], October 17–21, 1842).
KAMPF, DER, 1919, articles by Fritz Adler.
MOUVEMENT SOCIALISTE, LE, November 1, 1904, article by Edouard Berth.
TIMES, THE, The Ferment of Revolution, September 25, 1917, et seq.
WORKER, THE (SCOTTISH), article by J. R. White, Does Knowledge Precede · Action ? September 27, 1919.
Socialist press passim.

BRIGHT, JOHN, Speech on the Irish Question, Birmingham, November 16, 1880.
HERZEN, ALEXANDER, Letter to Michelet 1851 (quoted by Masaryk, see above, vol. i, p. 412).
POTTIER, EUGÈNE, The International, translated from the French by Eden and Cedar Paul, L.W.C.

Printed in Great Britain by
UNWIN BROTHERS LIMITED, THE GRESHAM PRESS, WOKING AND LONDON